Gulf of Mexico
Miami
Florida Keys
Straits of Florida
BAHAMAS
La Habana
(Havana)
José Martí
Intl Airport
Lourdes
Communications
Facility
CUBA
Santa
Clara
Greater
Guantanamo
U.S. Naval
Air Station,
Guantanamo Bay
Straits
of
Florida
Bahía de
La Habana
La Habana
(Havana)
Lourdes
Communications
Facility
José Martí
International
Airport
Bejucal
Montego
Bay
JAMAICA
Kingston
HAIT
Pedro
Cays
HONDURAS
Caribb
NICARAGUA
Bluefields
Bahía
Punta Gorda
Santa
Marta
Barranquilla
Cartagena
COSTA
RICA
Puerto
Limón
Colón
Panama
Canal
Golfo de Los
Mosquitos
Golfo
de
Uraba
Panama
PANAMA
COLOMB

SMARTS

SMARTS

Are We Hardwired for Success?

CHUCK MARTIN

PEG DAWSON, ED.D.

RICHARD GUARE, Ph.D.

AMACOM AMERICAN MANAGEMENT ASSOCIATION
New York • Atlanta • Brussels • Chicago • Mexico City
San Francisco • Shanghai • Tokyo • Toronto • Washington, D.C.

Special discounts on bulk quantities of AMACOM books are available to corporations, professional associations, and other organizations. For details, contact Special Sales Department, AMACOM, a division of American Management Association, 1601 Broadway, New York, NY 10019.
Tel: 212-903-8316. Fax: 212-903-8083.
E-mail: specialsls@amanet.org
Website: www.amacombooks.org/go/specialsales
To view all AMACOM titles go to: www.amacombooks.org

This publication is designed to provide accurate and authoritative information in regard to the subject matter covered. It is sold with the understanding that the publisher is not engaged in rendering legal, accounting, or other professional service. If legal advice or other expert assistance is required, the services of a competent professional person should be sought.

Library of Congress Cataloging-in-Publication Data

Martin, Chuck, 1949–
    Smarts : are we hardwired for success? / Chuck Martin Peg Dawson, Richard Guare.
        p.   cm.
    Includes bibliographical references and index.
    ISBN-10 0-8144-0906-7
    ISBN-13: 978-0-8144-0906-0
    1. Executive ability—Testing.   I. Dawson, Peg.   II. Guare, Richard.   III. Title.

HD38.2.M3675   2007
658.4'09—dc22

                                                                        2006029750

Printing number

10   9   8   7   6   5   4   3   2   1

To Teri, my wife, and Ryan and Chase, my sons, for the understanding, space, and total support you constantly provide.

—Chuck Martin

To Steven, who thinks all his Executive Skills are perfect—and I love him anyway!

—Peg Dawson

To my wife, Megan, and my children, Colin and Shannon, for their never-ending patience and willingness to lend their frontal lobes when mine go missing.

—Richard Guare

CONTENTS

ACKNOWLEDGMENTS

There are many people we want to acknowledge and thank for their assistance along the way to the final completion of this book.

We want to thank the members of NFI Research, the 2,000 senior executives and managers around the globe who answer our bimonthly surveys and take their precious time to convey to us their thoughts on the leading business and workplace issues of the day. We especially want to thank the VIP members, those who go above and beyond and provide us with even more feedback and guidance.

A sincere thank you to those executives and managers who reviewed the first draft manuscript and provided insightful feedback and suggestions on the content. Thanks for this effort go to Fred Becker, Al Blazek, Ken Myers, Ed Pease, Dave Schmidgall, Tim Smith, Robert Wyatt, Peter Eder, John Ogrizovich, Michel Beaulieu, Youri Lamoureux, Jim Moore, David Aschenbach, Carolyn Dickson, John Jarvis, Bill McBride, Terry Sullivan, and Brad Stephen.

Although many people have contributed to the refinement of the thinking in this book, we are especially grateful for the many hours of discussion and insights about the application of these ideas to the business world to Dr. Derek Stern, Janet Eastman, and Barry Nelson; and to Eleanor Guare, who deserves a special thanks for providing her experience and expertise to help validate many of our strategies.

We want to acknowledge Kevin Grady and Kyle Sevits, research directors of NFI Research, for conducting the worldwide surveys for the book, and NFI Research marketing and publicity directors Jeff Blake and Jamie Adams, for checking the manuscript and helping spread the word of our findings.

We are especially grateful to Jacquie Flynn, our editor at AMACOM, who not only immediately grasped the concepts of the book and helped us shape it, but also now practices the concepts in her day-to-day work.

All direct quotes in the book are based on interviews personally conducted by author Chuck Martin. Thank you to all those executives and managers who took the time to share their thinking.

SMARTS

Introduction

YOU MAY CONSIDER YOURSELF to be an organized person, or a procrastinator, or sometimes forgetful. Maybe you see yourself as someone who can get things done, or is highly flexible, cool under pressure, or good at managing your time. Although you might be accurate in some of your self-assessment, there has been no way to precisely define each of these attributes, or to show their relationship to each other.

These are actually brain functions or cognitive skills that neuroscientists have located in specific regions of the brain—primarily the frontal lobes. These functions develop starting at birth and they are *hardwired* into every individual. Brain researchers have found that these skills are fully developed by the time you become an adult.

These skills are called *Executive Skills* because they help you *execute* tasks. Executive Skills help you make decisions about what information you should focus on—both what's worth dealing with and what should be ignored—and they help independently manage your own behavior. They temper and adjust your emotions, help you review and modify your actions, and fine-tune your response as you move from one issue or activity to the next.

You can clearly and easily identify your strongest and weakest Executive Skills to enable you to play to those strengths while minimizing weaknesses. Your strongest Executive Skills will continue to be your strongest and your weakest will continue to be your weakest, because they are not dramatically changeable by the time you become an adult. The opportunity is in how you deal with them, and this book provides a framework for you to do that. You will learn why you—and those around you—act or behave the way you do. We provide strategies, approaches, and tactics to use these functions effectively.

Although researchers have different ways of labeling, defining, and organizing Executive Skills, our model encompasses twelve separate Executive Skills that are most relevant to the way people function in a work environment.

Despite the term "Executive Skills," whose use in neuropsychology dates back decades, there is no connection to executives at work. Executive Skills should not be confused with "skills of executives," since Executive Skills are, in fact, how the frontal lobes and associated brain areas manage information and behavior.

Each of you has a set of strongest and weakest Executive Skills in your own makeup. Generally, you have two or three that are strongest and two or three that are weakest. Those in the middle are not likely to get you in trouble, though they cannot be dramatically improved either.

Everyone has this personal combination of Executive Skills strengths and weaknesses, and they vary from person to person. Once you recognize and understand these skills, you can leverage them to get yourself into situations to use the strongest ones, while avoiding or minimizing those that are weakest.

Matching Strengths to the Situation

Using knowledge of your Executive Skills strengths, you can identify jobs that can play to those strengths. By identifying your key weaknesses, you also can avoid situations that are likely to result in failure. Everyone has seen or experienced this in one form or another:

- An extremely successful person gets what looks like a logical promotion and then ultimately fails in the new job.

- A friend regularly says the first thing that pops into his mind, often causing awkward foot-in-mouth moments.

- A person who was miserable and failing at a job in one company leaves and becomes wildly successful at another.

- A manager is constantly dissatisfied that an employee cannot seem to complete a task that seems so easy to the manager.

- A company names five of its smartest people to develop a new product, and it never gets off the ground.

In each case, there was a mismatch between the person and the skills the situation required. More critically, each outcome could have been predicted. A person's set of Executive Skills helps determine why people succeed and fail. In some situations, people excel because their Executive Skills strengths are a perfect fit to the task or situation. In others, they fail because they are anything but a perfect fit.

The basis for determining a person's strengths and weaknesses in Executive Skills is well grounded in neuropsychology and revolves around these fixed functions associated with the frontal lobes. Psychologists have been using knowledge of the development of these functions from childhood through adolescence to provide guidelines for assessment and assistance to children and teens. However, until now no one has taken this knowledge to the next level: helping adults use knowledge about these fixed skills for work and life. That is what we attempt to do with *Smarts.*

Since the strengths or weaknesses of these skills cannot be changed in a major way, there is a great opportunity for you or anyone else to tap into those that are strongest in all aspects of work. By leveraging the strongest parts of your Executive Skills, you can continually create situations where you and the task at hand achieve a more perfect fit. Throughout the book, we attempt to be as specific as possible regarding how Executive Skills strengths can map to specific tasks.

Once you determine your own set of Executive Skills, you can benchmark those against any given task, situation, or even a job, which might explain why you are succeeding or failing, and what the future may hold. You also can identify these strengths and weaknesses in others, allowing you to fit better, manage better, build more effective teams, and better match people to the right jobs.

The Executive Skills

We have identified twelve brain-based Executive Skills that are developed by young adulthood and are critical for decision making and regulation of behavior. They are:

1. *Self-Restraint*: The ability to think before you act. It is the ability to resist the urge to say or do something to allow time to evaluate the situation and how a behavior might affect it.

2. *Working Memory*: The ability to hold information in memory while performing complex tasks. It involves drawing on past learning or experience to apply to the situation at hand or to project into the future.

3. *Emotion Control*: The ability to manage emotions in order to achieve goals, complete tasks, or control and direct behavior.

4. *Focus*: The capacity to maintain attention to a situation or task in spite of distractibility, fatigue, or boredom.

5. *Task Initiation*: The ability to begin projects or tasks without undue procrastination.

6. *Planning and Prioritization*: The capacity to develop a road map to arrive at a destination or goal, and knowing which are the most important signposts along the way.

7. *Organization*: The ability to arrange or place according to a system.

8. *Time Management*: The capacity to estimate how much time one has, to allocate it effectively, and to stay within time limits and deadlines. It involves a sense that time is important.

9. *Defining and Achieving Goals*: The capacity to have a goal, follow through to the completion of the goal, and not be put off or distracted by competing interests along the way.

10. *Flexibility*: The ability to revise plans in the face of obstacles, setbacks, new information, or mistakes. It relates to adaptability to changing conditions.

11. *Observation*: The capacity to stand back and take a birds-eye view of yourself in a situation and to be able to understand and make changes in the ways that you solve problems.

12. *Stress Tolerance*: The ability to thrive in stressful situations and to cope with uncertainty, change, and performance demands.

The Benefits of Understanding Executive Skills

The effects of understanding Executive Skill strengths and weaknesses are enormous for individuals and for entire organizations. Aligning your strengths with the jobs, tasks, or teams that best use those strengths presents a winning combination. When an organization does this as a matter of course, there are number of positive benefits across the company:

- *Productivity*: The right matches increase the chances of tasks being accomplished faster. With the right person in the right job, that job can be managed with less effort. This results in less time being spent on activities, freeing people to increase their personal output. The proper mix of people in the right jobs also means more deadlines being met, since the people are, in effect, better able to complete the tasks at hand.

- *Quality*: Matching the right people to the right jobs increases the likelihood that there will be fewer errors, since the tasks being performed are inherently natural for those individuals.

- *Employee Recruitment*: Getting the right people in the right job will be easier because the Executive Skills profile of the job can be matched against potential candidates for the job. Matching a person's strengths to the strengths required for a job can assure a better fit.

■ *Employee Retention*: Employees and managers doing tasks that best match their skills are happier and less likely to look for a job elsewhere. If this is done on a wide scale, there is likely to be less tension in the workplace as well, with people actually looking forward to doing their jobs.

■ *Training*: By knowing that a person's Executive Skills strengths and weaknesses cannot be dramatically changed, we can focus training more on enabling people to learn how to identify and leverage their strengths and work around their weaknesses. Even better, training will not be wasted on unsuccessfully trying to improve a person's greatest weaknesses through training classes.

■ *Teamwork*: Members of teams at all levels can be properly matched with each other, assuring a more effective work process, better results, and less conflict along the way.

■ *Competitive Edge*: Correctly matching people and jobs provides an organization with at least a short-term competitive advantage. Although much of the matching activities can be duplicated, it would require a detailed analysis of most employees and a reengineering of a number of people-related processes to catch up to a business that started early. However, an organization only has to go through this process one time, and it can be over a period of time to reduce disruption of the business. But the business that starts first has the advantage.

■ *Stress*: With people better matched to their jobs, the toll on individuals performing inherently difficult day-to-day activities will be reduced.

■ *Meetings*: The right people at the right meetings will increase efficiency and more accurately predict meeting outcomes. Having the proper combination of Executive Skills strengths at a meeting will assure that the results will be the correct results and also ones that are realistically achievable. With the right people with the right Executive Skills responsible, more meetings will start and end on time.

■ *Execution*: When an organization has people playing to their Executive Skills strengths, the ideas or strategies will be developed by the right people in combination with the right people who can keep tabs on what can be done within a reasonable time frame.

■ *Information Management*: With the right people in the right jobs, information flow will be more efficient because people will be dealing with only what is most relevant for their particular role in the organization. When people know their strengths, they can align the information flow to support those strengths, ignoring much of the rest.

Frontal Lobes and Executive Skills

The brain is a complex organ, and both neuropsychologists and writers for the popular press have attempted to paint a simplified picture—a line drawing, if you will—to help the public understand how it works and what part of the brain performs what function. Books have been written, for example, about left-brain and right-brain functions, with *language* being the skill most commonly attributed to the left brain, and *emotions* and *spatial concepts* being the domains most commonly attributed to the right brain. In fact, it is more complex than that (the tone of voice with which someone speaks, for instance, is interpreted by the right hemisphere of the brain, while the words themselves are interpreted by the left hemisphere).

More broadly, there are portions of the brain responsible for perception, memory, language, and movement. But for an individual *to do* anything with all that information requires the activation of the frontal lobes. The frontal lobes of the brain—the portion of the brain just behind the forehead—are responsible for reasoning and decision making. In terms of brain functioning, the frontal lobes and particularly the prefrontal cortex are almost unique in their ability to receive signals from all other brain regions, thus enabling them to factor in previous experiences and prior knowledge, current biological states, and incoming information from the external world. It is for this reason that the frontal lobes are sometimes called the *central executive*. And Executive Skills are the mechanisms by which humans sift through massive amounts of information in order to reason and make decisions.

The development of Executive Skills parallels the development of the brain. When a baby is born, the brain weighs about 13 ounces. By late adolescence, brain weight has increased to just under 3 pounds. Although all areas of the brain are growing, neuroscientists generally agree that the frontal brain systems, among the last to develop in late adolescence, play a preeminent role in Executive Skills.

Railroad Accident and Frontal Lobes

It was September 13, 1848 when Phineas Gage, the foreman of a railway construction crew, was working to prepare the bed for the Rutland and Burlington Railroad near Cavendish, Vermont. A freakish accidental explosion blew a tamping iron through his head. The tamping iron was nearly four feet long and weighed more than 13 pounds. It went in under Gage's left cheekbone and completely out through the top of his head, landing about 25 yards away. Though Gage was knocked over, he reportedly remained conscious, though most of the front part of the left side of his brain was destroyed. Gage survived and after hospitalization returned to his home in Lebanon, New Hampshire, ten weeks after the accident.

The next year, Gage felt strong enough to go back to work. However, how he functioned had changed so profoundly that his employers wouldn't give him his management job back. Formerly well-balanced and considered one of the company's most capable and efficient foremen, Gage had become fitful, irreverent, and grossly profane, showing little deference for his fellow workers. Formerly considered a smart businessman, Gage had become vacillating, unable to settle on any of the plans he devised for future action.

Gage never worked as a foreman again and ended up working in a livery stable of the Dartmouth Inn in Hanover, New Hampshire. In about 1859, Gage went to San Francisco to live with his mother and died in 1860, a dozen years after the accident.

In 1867, Gage's body was exhumed and his skull and the tamping iron were sent to what ultimately became the Warren Museum of the Medical School of Harvard University, where they were studied extensively.

In 1994, using x-rays and computer graphics, researchers determined the probable path of the flying rod through Gage's head. From the analysis, it became clear that the rod had damaged Gage's frontal lobes. The findings provided an explanation for the transformation of Gage's behavior because the effects in Gage were not unique: Other people with frontal lobe damage had exhibited personality changes that resembled Gage's.

Other patients with frontal lobe damage, either brought on by traumatic injury or disease, were able, like Gage, to remember facts and perform complicated calculations. But when it came to keeping commitments, being trustworthy, holding a job, or succeeding in marriage, they failed miserably. They couldn't plan for the future, and they couldn't see how their behavior affected their own lives or the lives of others. They were lacking the brain functions that are Executive Skills.

Although specific skills associated with the frontal lobes have long been described in scientific literature, the usage of the term Executive Function, or Executive Skills, is more recent, dating back to the 1980s. However, in spite of its relatively young age, the term is now commonly recognized in the neuroscientific literature and associated with frontal lobe activity.

Executive Skills vs. Personality

There's an entire industry devoted to helping people understand how different personality styles affect how they function in the workplace and in life in general. There have been numerous books written to help identify personality traits and strengths. Historically, the Myers-Briggs Type Indicator is probably the most widely used assessment instrument for determining personality. This approach, derived from a theory of personality type developed by Carl Jung, a student of Freud, is based on the notion that an individual's personality comprises four dimensions. These dimensions relate to:

1. How you are energized (introversion versus extraversion)

2. What kind of information you attend to (concrete stimuli versus intuition)

3. How you make decisions (using thoughts versus using feelings)

4. How you organize your world (order and structure versus flexibility and spontaneity)

Although there is some overlap between the Personality Type model and the Executive Skills model outlined in this book, there are some critical differences:

▪ Executive Skills are grounded in brain functions that have been demonstrated through research in the neurosciences to reside in specific brain locations and to become activated under predictable conditions. There is no such brain research to substantiate Psychological Type.

▪ Executive Skills map neatly onto the kinds of tasks, functions, and roles that people are expected to perform in the workplace—whether they are working on the lowest rung of the corporate ladder or have climbed all the way to the top.

This book focuses on Executive Skills rather than on other dimensions of brain functioning because it is this region of the brain that determines what you concentrate on, how you judge information, how you make decisions, and how well you execute those decisions.

By understanding your own specific set of Executive Skill strengths and weaknesses, you will be able to find greater job satisfaction, no matter at what level you work or in what capacity you are employed. We believe an understanding of Executive Skills will enable you to improve performance in concrete and measurable ways that will help both you and the organization for which you work achieve greater success and better meet long-term goals.

How to Use This Book

We have written this book for you, the businessperson. It doesn't matter what business, profession, or industry you're in. Executive Skills cut across them all because these skills are all hardwired into your brain. It doesn't matter whether your company is large or small, or whether you work independently. What matters are the many relationships surrounding Executive Skills. There are the relationships among the skills themselves, with your strongest sometimes appearing to be at odds with your weakest skill. There are the relationships between your Executive Skills and those of the people around you. There are the relationships between the Executive Skills of the manager and those of the employee, which can be in harmony or in conflict. And although we do not dwell on it in any detail, there are the relationships between your Executive Skills and those of your friends and family. As you will see, Executive Skills are with you all the time, whether at home or at work, on vacation, or raising or dealing with children. But *Smarts* is primarily designed to help you make the most of your Executive Skills in your world of work.

Because there are employees as well as managers of employees, we have included information in two specific chapters to show how to *manage* Executive Skills in others. However, whether you are the manager or the person being managed, you first should learn of your own personal Executive Skills strengths and weaknesses. The book is organized in a fashion to do that.

Chapter 1 describes in detail each of the 12 Executive Skills and includes the Executive Skills Profile self-assessment for you to identify your strongest and weakest skills. (The sixty questions are also listed in Appendix B in the back of the book, if you want to answer all the questions at one time.) It is essential that you clearly identify these skills before moving on to the rest of the book for several reasons. Because only your two or three strongest and weakest skills really matter, for much of the remainder of the book you can pay more attention when we discuss your specific strengths and weaknesses. However, don't totally ignore the skills that don't pertain to you, because you will see them displayed in people all around you.

We have found that once people become familiar with the 12 Executive Skills, they start to look at things in a whole new light. If you are an employee, you will start to notice the specific strengths of your superiors and those around you. Even more significantly, people's weaknesses will jump out at you as you begin to link their behaviors and actions back to specific Executive Skills, which eventually becomes second nature. For example, when someone is extremely testy under pressure and unable or unwilling to change course, you'll find yourself muttering to yourself: "Ah yes, low in Flexibility." Or, when a certain vice president is running a meeting, you know there's no point in showing up early because his weakness is Time Management.

It will be like this with all twelve skills. The more you become familiar with Executive Skills the more easily you will spot both the strengths and weaknesses of others. It also might tend to make you more accommodating, when you know that the weakness is hardwired into the people and that it is not their fault they are behaving the way they are. Even more interesting is that you will have the solution for how to change or adapt to that situation.

People who have become familiar with our work in Executive Skills have told us that they now understand why a former boss or colleague seemed to act totally irrationally in certain situations. We've heard from managers who now understand why someone working for them in the past didn't work out. They now realize they were lacking the specific Executive Skills needed at the time.

Once you've read this book, you will have an advantage over anyone you deal with at work who does not have the same understanding of Executive Skills as you. This book will arm you with the tools, tactics, and strategies to play to your Executive Skills strengths. It also will show you how to deal with your own weaknesses so that they don't get you in trouble. And it will show you how to interact with others who have the same strengths as well as those that are opposites.

Chapter 2 identifies the logical combinations of Executive Skills and shows why it is difficult for you to work in a job that requires skills that are among your weakest. We further identify the characteristics of each of the 12 Executive Skills. This is where you find out more about your strongest and weakest skills, which you identified in Chapter 1. This is where you will receive a more detailed description of your own profile. This is also where you can begin to see types of work (strategy, detail work, troubleshooting, etc.) that might suit you best.

In Chapter 3 you learn to play to your Executive Skills strengths, which we believe is your best approach for dealing with your Executive Skills. Part of the process is to benchmark the Executive Skills strengths required in a job, task, or situation. We provide a quick table for you to identify the level of Executive Skill required and a place for you to compare your strengths. This is where we discuss how to leverage your strengths in team situations and in meetings. We also show you how to interview for jobs, with the emphasis on asking questions that will show whether the job will be a good fit for you before you pursue it.

Chapter 4 deals with your weaknesses and what to do about them. Although we strongly recommend you play to your Executive Skills strengths, there are methods to minimize your weaknesses, at least to the point that they don't get in your way. We have found that what is often perceived as poor communication can be directly traced to Executive Skills weaknesses, and we show you how to identify that. There are specific steps to take for a weakness in each of the 12 Executive Skills, so this is where you take the two or three weakest skills you identified in Chapter 1 and match them to the solution. Although the skill cannot be appreciably changed, the problems it causes can be tackled head-on.

Chapters 5 and 6 are squarely aimed at executives and managers to show how to manage Executive Skills in others. If you are a manager, this is where you'll see what steps should be taken to modify a behavior, or to change a situation so the behavior is no longer an issue. If you're not a manager, you still should read these chapters so that you will see organizational changes that you could instigate for yourself if your superior is unaware of Executive Skills and issues they cause. Chapter 6 provides a process to select the right people for the right jobs. Although this is targeted at managers, an employee or anyone looking for another job can gain knowledge of the matching process.

Chapter 7 is about alignment of your personal Executive Skills strengths with those of the organization for whom you work. This is where we match Executive Skills with specific job activities, including marketing, sales, customer service, and creativity. This is also where we discuss Executive Skills alignment as a career strategy for you.

The final chapter, Chapter 8, deals with outside forces that can cause your Executive Skills to effectively break down. We provide tactics to deal with such issues as e-mail overload, working too many hours, and challenging deadlines.

Background

Many of the strategies and tactics for identifying and dealing with Executive Skills strengths and weaknesses come from more than twenty years of clinical work with people who have Executive Skills deficits. It is this clinical work that led to an understanding of how Executive Skills develop and how they affect learning and performance.

The strategies have been refined and modified during more than ten years of training sessions and seminars that were conducted by two of the authors (Peg Dawson and Richard Guare) and attended by psychologists, rehabilitation specialists, teachers, doctors, and parents. The objective of these sessions has been to reduce the impact of Executive Skills weaknesses. In the process of conducting this training, we developed an assessment tool to help adults identify their own Executive Skills strengths and weaknesses and to understand how they can modify their work or their work environment to better match their strengths to the work that they do.

Throughout this book, you also will see surveys that deal with topics ranging from specific Executive Skills to how managers deal with weaknesses in others. These surveys were conducted by NFI Research exclusively for this book to help validate and highlight some of the issues in the workplace specifically related to Executive Skills. NFI Research is a U.S.-based research organization that has surveyed 2,000 senior executives and managers globally every two weeks for eight years. It has chronicled the transformation of business and countless workplace issues. It was started by one of the authors (Chuck Martin) as a way to keep in touch with executives and managers the author has addressed in lectures throughout the world and to identify, monitor, and analyze trends in business. Respondents were asked to write additional comments, many of which have been included in the book under the headings "Voices from the Front Lines."

Using What You Have

We intend through this book to effectively arm you with information, systems, processes, and templates to help you fully use your Executive Skills. If you are a manager, we will show you how to fill in gaps of subordinates' Executive Skills by changing the situation or the context in which certain activities are performed. But in all cases, we will show you how to tap into your greatest Executive Skills strengths and to best use what you've got, which is what *Smarts* is all about.

∎

For updates and comments, we invite you to visit **www.smartsthebook .com.**

Taking Inventory with the Executive Skills Profile

THE FIRST STEP in determining your combinations of strengths and weaknesses is to measure each of your 12 Executive Skills. Everyone has strengths and everyone has weaknesses in their skills. It would be extremely unusual for a person to be strong in all twelve skills, since some are effectively opposites. There are some common combinations of strengths and weaknesses, so that people who are strong in specific skills are often weak in certain others, and the patterns are predictable.

Determining your strongest and weakest skill requires that you understand each of the skills and the characteristics associated with them. Several of the Executive Skills in which you excel or fail will be obvious to you right away. For example, you probably already know whether you are good at starting projects easily without procrastinating. Or you might feel that you are generally flexible or inflexible.

However, the key is to understand all of your 12 Executive Skills in relation to each other, after measuring the strength and weakness of each. This will reveal to you combinations from which you can move forward. You can help determine your Executive Skills strengths by answering a small set of questions for each of the skills, which will highlight your highest (strongest) and lowest (weakest) skills.

People typically have two or three strengths and two or three weaknesses, with the remaining Executive Skills falling somewhere between. Those that are in between are not generally likely to get you in trouble, but those at the extremes can help you position yourself for greater successes and fewer failures. Those that are strongest will allow you to determine what tasks, projects, relationships, and even careers you would find yourself comfortably matched to. Those that are weakest can show you personal situations and even jobs and careers that you should avoid. In Chapters 3 and 4 we will describe how you can improve your strongest skills and ways to work around or complement those that are weakest.

As every executive, manager, and employee knows, it is easy to lie on a questionnaire that is being used for self-evaluation, and the self-assessment questions in this chapter are no exception. However, Executive Skills strengths and weaknesses are real and are imbedded in your brain. So answering a set of questions in a way that makes you look strong in an Executive Skill does not make you strong in that skill, and you most likely will know it. Additionally, there are people who delude themselves into thinking they are good at virtually everything, and they may tend to rate themselves high across the board. In clinical psychology, there is a term for intentionally viewing oneself in only positive terms in virtually every aspect across the board; it is called *faking good*. A person who is *faking good* will have difficulty admitting weaknesses.

In answering questions there also is the rare possibility of subconsciously answering positively across the board. This is called *symptom magnification*. In this case, it would be called *Executive Skills magnification*, if all scores are unintentionally inflated. An indication of this would be high scores across the board when tallying the final result. Should you end up with all high scores, ask someone who knows you well to answer the questions about you, and then compare your answers to look for discrepancies. (For readers who want to answer all the questions at one time, the self-assessment questions are also listed in Appendix B in the back of the book.)

Skill 1: Self-Restraint

Everyone knows someone who always seems to put the proverbial foot in the mouth. This could be from a lack of Self-Restraint, the Executive Skill that involves the ability to resist the urge to say or do something while allowing time to evaluate the situation you're in and how what you say or do might affect that situation.

This Executive Skill is about having the capacity to think before speaking or acting. Often it is what someone says that causes you to want to respond. It might be a discussion where your spouse casually mentions a person who is not in the room, and you quickly blurt out that she is a real jerk, within earshot of others who are her friends. Or it may be your boss, who takes his golf seriously, mentioning how well he did in his game over the weekend, and you immediately say you think golf is such a waste of time.

If you lean to informed decision making, generally take a methodical and deliberate approach to things, and are not often impulsive, you probably are high in self-restraint. You also could easily suppress a response until you've thought about it.

On the other hand, if you often act on impulse, tend to say the first thing that pops into your mind, and generally act before you consider the consequences, you probably are low in this skill. If you can easily remember a few things you said that you later regretted, that is a clue that self-restraint is not one of your strongest Executive Skills. Another clue is if you often feel like you want to kick yourself for what you just said. If you often want to kick someone *else* for what they just said, they may be low in Self-Restraint.

Another way to determine whether this skill is high or low for you is to recall how you've acted in past situations to determine whether you actually *use* this skill. For example, you would be using this skill when you worked around the clock finishing a project for a demanding client, who then says he's not happy with your work, and you answer him without losing your temper. Or when your boss suggests a bold, new initiative that looks good on the surface, you suggest assembling a meeting to discuss the pros and cons of doing it. (There are, of course, rare cases when that boss might say something to intentionally make you uncomfortable just to cause a specific reaction, which is not really a Self-Restraint issue.)

Self-Restraint Questions

Read each item below and then rate the item based on the extent to which you agree or disagree with how well it describes you. Use the 5-point scoring system to choose the appropriate score for each statement. Then add the five scores for your total.

	Strongly Disagree	Somewhat Disagree	Neither Agree nor Disagree	Somewhat Agree	Strongly Agree
I take my time before making up my mind	1	2	3	4	5
I see myself as tactful and diplomatic	1	2	3	4	5
I think before I speak	1	2	3	4	5
I make sure I have all the facts before I take action	1	2	3	4	5
I seldom make comments that make people uncomfortable	1	2	3	4	5

Total Score _____

Skill 2: Working Memory

If you never use a list to go shopping and always get what you need, you're probably high in Working Memory. This is more than only recalling something from the past. It's as if your memory is always *on*, no matter how busy you are or what you're doing. Working Memory involves the ability to hold information in memory while performing complex tasks. It involves drawing on past learning or experience to apply to the situation at hand or to project into the future.

When you remember that you promised to get to your son's soccer game at 4 P.M. in the midst of an emergency that pops up at the office at 1 P.M. you are using the skill of Working Memory. If you're usually able to do one task and not lose sight of other commitments, you probably are high in Working Memory. You also would be considered reliable, can be counted on to follow through, and able to keep your eye on the ball.

You'd be using this skill when you remember to return an expense report your assistant asked for when you're working on a tight budget deadline. Or you remember you have a dentist appointment when you call the service station to fix your unexpected flat tire.

On the other hand, if you're sometimes absent-minded and need frequent reminders to complete tasks, you're probably low in Working Memory. You would be likely to miss an appointment because you didn't write it down, or you might leave your cell phone on your airline seat because you were worried about making a tight connection. You might also have forgotten that a week ago you promised to meet your spouse for lunch today because something pressing came up at work late this morning.

Working Memory Questions

Rate each item based on the extent to which you agree or disagree with how well it describes you.

	Strongly Disagree	Somewhat Disagree	Neither Agree nor Disagree	Somewhat Agree	Strongly Agree
I have a good memory for facts, dates, and details	1	2	3	4	5
I am good at remembering the things that I have committed to do	1	2	3	4	5
I very naturally remember to complete tasks	1	2	3	4	5
I keep sight of goals that I want to accomplish	1	2	3	4	5
When I'm busy, I keep track of both the big picture and the details	1	2	3	4	5

Total Score _____

Skill 3: Emotion Control

If you can keep your emotions in check to the point that they don't get in the way of what you're trying to do, you're probably high in Emotion Control, which is the ability to manage emotions in order to achieve goals, complete tasks, or control and direct behavior. It involves making positive statements to yourself, suppressing negative self-statements, and even delaying immediate gratification while you pursue more important long-term goals.

If you're high in Emotion Control, you would not be easily side-tracked, would tend to get the job done, be unemotional and cool under pressure, be able to resist temptations that might lead you astray, not easily be discouraged, and be resilient in the face of setbacks. If you are high in Emotion Control, you would tend to find something positive in a negative performance review, be able to bounce back after an emotional upset, and be able to psych yourself up to make a phone call you dread.

If you're low in Emotion Control, you can be overly emotional and sensitive to criticism. If you're not using this skill, you might go into a situation expecting to fail, tell yourself this is the worst presentation you've ever done, or find yourself dwelling all day on criticism you received in the morning. A common sign of low Emotion Control is having difficulty controlling anger, irritability, and frustration.

Emotion Control Questions

Rate each item based on the extent to which you agree or disagree with how well it describes you.

	Strongly Disagree	Somewhat Disagree	Neither Agree nor Disagree	Somewhat Agree	Strongly Agree
I can keep my emotions in check when on the job	1	2	3	4	5
I usually handle confrontations calmly	1	2	3	4	5
Little things don't affect me emotionally and distract me from the task at hand	1	2	3	4	5
When frustrated or angry, I keep my cool	1	2	3	4	5
I easily defer my personal feelings until after a task has been completed	1	2	3	4	5

Total Score _____

Skill 4: Focus

The Executive Skill of Focus is about having the ability to stick with something. It is the capacity to maintain attention to a situation or task.

If you're high in Focus, you find it easy to stay on the task at hand, become immersed in that task, and can screen out distractions. Even though you're tired at the end of a day, you would rather complete that report you're writing because you know it will be easier to finish it now instead of beginning again the next day. You have a reputation for making deadlines because you can stick with things. Focus is having the capacity to maintain attention to a situation or task in spite of distractions, fatigue, or boredom.

If you have a low score in Focus, you have difficulty seeing things through to the end, and can be easily distracted. For example, someone low in Focus might have a performance review due in less than an hour but decide to check e-mail first. Or they might take work home to do over the weekend but save it for Sunday night, when they get sidetracked by a football game on television.

Focus Questions
Rate each item based on the extent to which you agree or disagree with how well it describes you.

	Strongly Disagree	Somewhat Disagree	Neither Agree nor Disagree	Somewhat Agree	Strongly Agree
When I have a job to do or task to finish, I easily avoid distractions	1	2	3	4	5
Once I start an assignment, I work diligently until it is completed	1	2	3	4	5
I find it easy to stay focused on my work	1	2	3	4	5
Even when interrupted, I get back to work to complete the job at hand	1	2	3	4	5
I attend to a task even when I find it somewhat tedious	1	2	3	4	5

Total Score _____

Skill 5: Task Initiation
If you tend to do something today rather than put it off until tomorrow, you're probably high in Task Initiation, which is the ability to begin tasks or projects without procrastinating. Getting started on something would come easy for you, with an action-orientation and propensity to get the job going without undue delay, in an efficient or timely fashion.

You would tend to pay your bills as soon as you receive them and immediately tackle that project that is due in four weeks. You begin a task when you promised you would and generally hit the ground running as soon as you get to work.

If you're low in the skill of Task Initiation, you probably tend to procrastinate and be slow getting started on projects. You might seek that extra cup of coffee before getting down to work. You would also frequently (and well intentionally) prefer to start something tomorrow rather than today.

Task Initiation Questions

Rate the item based on the extent to which you agree or disagree with how well it describes you.

	Strongly Disagree	Somewhat Disagree	Neither Agree nor Disagree	Somewhat Agree	Strongly Agree
Once I've been given a job or task, I like to start it immediately	1	2	3	4	5
Procrastination is usually not a problem for me	1	2	3	4	5
No matter what the task, I believe in getting started as soon as possible	1	2	3	4	5
I can get right to work even if there's something I'd rather be doing	1	2	3	4	5
I generally start tasks early	1	2	3	4	5

Total Score _____

Skill 6: Planning/Prioritization

If you are high in this Executive Skill, you're well organized, efficient, and clear thinking. You probably make a list of steps required to complete a project and easily say no to a colleague's request for help if it means you can't finish your own project that's on a tight deadline. Planning/Prioritization is the ability to create a roadmap to reach a goal. You're also able to decide between two courses of action based on the potential benefits of each. Planning/Prioritization involves being able to make decisions about what's important to focus on and what's not. It is the ability to identify and organize the steps needed to carry out your intentions or achieve a goal.

If you're low in this skill, you might not be sure where to start and be unsure of what's important, and can't seem to make plans. You tend to drop a well-thought-out project because a great new idea just presented itself or your subordinates keep coming to you asking what they should do next. At the end of the day, you have no clear idea of how you will spend the next day.

Planning/Prioritization Questions

Rate the item based on the extent to which you agree or disagree with how well it describes you.

	Strongly Disagree	Somewhat Disagree	Neither Agree nor Disagree	Somewhat Agree	Strongly Agree
When I start my day, I have a clear plan in mind for what I hope to accomplish	1	2	3	4	5
When I have a lot to do, I focus on the most important things	1	2	3	4	5
I have formulated plans to achieve my most important long-term goals	1	2	3	4	5
I am good at identifying priorities and sticking to them	1	2	3	4	5
I typically break big tasks down into subtasks and timelines	1	2	3	4	5

Total Score _____

Skill 7: Organization

An easy clue to whether you are high in Organization is how well you keep track of your belongings. If you're inclined to be neat and pay attention to detail, you most likely are high in Organization, which is the ability to arrange according to a system. If your desk is generally tidy (and you naturally like it that way) and there are no piles of paper waiting to be filed, you probably are high in Organization.

On the other hand, if you are low in Organization, you are somewhat messy and routinely misplace or lose things. You do not maintain systems for organizing information, such as files, e-mail, or your in-box. You rely on others to find things you have misplaced.

Organization Questions
Rate each item based on the extent to which you agree or disagree with how well it describes you.

	Strongly Disagree	Somewhat Disagree	Neither Agree nor Disagree	Somewhat Agree	Strongly Agree
I am an organized person	1	2	3	4	5
I am good at maintaining systems for organizing my work	1	2	3	4	5
It is natural for me to keep my work area neat and organized	1	2	3	4	5
It is easy for me to keep track of my materials	1	2	3	4	5
It is easy for me to organize things, such as e-mail, in-box, and to-do items	1	2	3	4	5

Total Score _____

Skill 8: Time Management

If you're high in the Executive Skill of Time Management you tend to be efficient, able to meet deadlines, and methodical. When someone asks you how long it will take to complete a project you can estimate the correct time within 90 percent accuracy. In the course of a day, you can juggle the tasks you need to accomplish so that most get completed and those that don't are the least important. Time Management is the capacity to estimate how much time one has, to allocate it, and to stay within time limits and deadlines. It involves a sense that time is important.

If you are low in Time Management, you have difficulty meeting deadlines. The meetings you run don't start on time, run late, or often both. At the end of the day, you realize you didn't get done half of what you had planned because you consistently underestimated the amount of time it took to do something.

Time Management Questions
Rate each item based on the extent to which you agree or disagree with how well it describes you.

	Strongly Disagree	Somewhat Disagree	Neither Agree nor Disagree	Somewhat Agree	Strongly Agree
I pace myself according to the time demands of a task	1	2	3	4	5
At the end of the day, I've usually finished what I set out to do	1	2	3	4	5
I am good at estimating how long it takes to do something	1	2	3	4	5
I am usually on time for appointments and activities	1	2	3	4	5
I routinely set and follow a daily schedule of activities	1	2	3	4	5

Total Score _____

Skill 9: Defining and Achieving Goals

If you succeed in most of the goals you set for yourself, you probably are high in the Executive Skill of Defining and Achieving Goals, which is the capacity to have a goal and follow through with actions to achieve it. You tend to be task focused, can be expected to complete tasks you take on, and are able to achieve long-term goals. You don't let obstacles get in your way and always keep your eye on the ball, despite efforts of those around you to draw you into activities unrelated to what you're trying to accomplish. You have the capacity to have a goal, follow through to the completion of the goal, and not be put off or distracted by competing interests.

If you tend to be controlled by the present, can't focus beyond the short term, and lose sight of objectives, you probably are low in Defining and Achieving Goals. You typically can't say "no" to opportunities that pass your way, even when they prevent you from accomplishing important goals in a timely manner. You get excited by new ideas but can't seem to see them come to fruition.

Defining and Achieving Goals Questions

Rate each item based on the extent to which you agree or disagree with how well it describes you.

	Strongly Disagree	Somewhat Disagree	Neither Agree nor Disagree	Somewhat Agree	Strongly Agree
When I encounter an obstacle, I still achieve my goal	1	2	3	4	5
I think of myself as being driven to meet my goals	1	2	3	4	5
I am good at achieving high levels of performance	1	2	3	4	5
I have a good ability to set long-term goals	1	2	3	4	5
I easily give up immediate pleasures while working on long-term goals	1	2	3	4	5

Total Score _____

Skill 10: Flexibility

A high score in Flexibility implies you are independent, able to integrate new information, adaptable and able to change course, and able to act autonomously. When your flight is canceled, you quickly work out alternative travel arrangements. When the overnight package needed for a meeting that day isn't delivered, you determine the best way to handle the situation without panic. You can re-do a presentation when an associate calls in sick at the last minute, and you can handle going back to school because your daughter left her homework assignment there. You have the ability to revise plans in the face of obstacles, setbacks, new information, or mistakes.

Flexibility is the ability to revise plans, and it relates to the amount of adaptability one has to changing conditions. It involves the capacity to generate an alternative plan when confronted with obstacles or new information.

A low degree of Flexibility would make you less adaptable to change with a lack of willingness to incorporate new information. Once you've decided on a plan, you're not comfortable changing it or seeing alternatives. You tend to panic when your car won't start because you have an important meeting coming up, and you might get rattled when your boss asks you to make a change in your travel plans, just after completing them with the travel agent. You are put out when someone calls while you are washing your car or the supermarket is out of a key ingredient you need for a planned dinner.

Flexibility Questions

Rate each item based on the extent to which you agree or disagree with how well it describes you.

	Strongly Disagree	Somewhat Disagree	Neither Agree nor Disagree	Somewhat Agree	Strongly Agree
I consider myself to be flexible and adaptive to change	1	2	3	4	5
I generally see different ways to address or attack a problem	1	2	3	4	5
I take unexpected events in stride	1	2	3	4	5
I easily can view situations from the perspective of other people	1	2	3	4	5
I think well on my feet	1	2	3	4	5

Total Score _____

Skill 11: Observation

If you're self-reflective, think strategically, and are able to observe your own actions as well as group processes impartially, you probably are high in the skill of Observation, which is the ability to stand back and take a birds-eye view of yourself or others in a situation and be able to understand and make changes in how you solve problems. It is an ability to observe how you problem-solve. It also includes self-monitoring and self-evaluative skills, such as asking yourself, "How am I doing?" or "How did I do?" If you are high in Observation, you can figure out multiple solutions to a problem, analyze the pros and cons, and select the one you think will work best. You can step back and figure out what went wrong in a failed presentation and can easily imagine the threats and opportunities of a new business opportunity.

A low skill of Observation means you do not think through the implications of decisions. You might be inclined to shoot from the hip, miss seeing the big picture, and tend to repeat the same mistakes. You make decisions based on what feels right and can make snap decisions about something that has long-term consequences you never thought of. You use the same approach to a problem even though that approach didn't work the last three times you used it. A clue if you are low in Observation is if people around you get annoyed with you for not being able to see what's important.

Observation Questions

Rate each item based on the extent to which you agree or disagree with how well it describes you.

	Strongly Disagree	Somewhat Disagree	Neither Agree nor Disagree	Somewhat Agree	Strongly Agree
I easily recognize when a task is a good match for my skills and abilities	1	2	3	4	5
I routinely evaluate my performance and devise methods for personal improvement	1	2	3	4	5
I generally step back from a situation in order to make objective decisions	1	2	3	4	5
I enjoy strategic thinking and sound problem solving	1	2	3	4	5
I can review a situation and see where I could have done things differently	1	2	3	4	5

Total Score _____

Skill 12: Stress Tolerance

If you thrive on the subjective feeling of stress and maintain control in pressure situations, you probably are high in Stress Tolerance, which is the ability to thrive in stressful situations and to cope with uncertainty, change, and performance demands.

You would have a high tolerance for ambiguity and be emotionally steady in a crisis. You can handle a deadline being moved up and even welcome the challenge of working through the night to finish it. Your three children all have events the same evening and you take in stride that you have to get them to different locations on time.

A low level of Stress Tolerance would make you emotionally stressed in a crisis. You only feel comfortable when you know your schedule for the next few weeks. If you make an error in a presentation you are likely to obsess about it for days. You get angry when the boss asks you to divert from your current task in favor of another, or when your spouse asks you stop at a store on the way home just when you got on the highway.

Stress Tolerance Questions

Rate each item based on the extent to which you agree or disagree with how well it describes you.

	Strongly Disagree	Somewhat Disagree	Neither Agree nor Disagree	Somewhat Agree	Strongly Agree
I enjoy working in a highly demanding, fast-paced environment	1	2	3	4	5
Pressure helps me perform at my best	1	2	3	4	5
Jobs that include a fair degree of unpredictability appeal to me	1	2	3	4	5
I am comfortable taking risks when the situation calls for it	1	2	3	4	5
I like jobs where there are not many set schedules	1	2	3	4	5

Total Score ———

Your Unique Set of Executive Skills

After you've finished this chapter and answered all the questions, go back and find your two or three highest and the two or three lowest scores. Those will be your strongest and weakest Executive Skills. The answers to the self-assessment provide your unique set of Executive Skills strengths and weaknesses. Your strengths and weaknesses are in relation to each other. So if you scored, for example, an 18 in Observation and someone you know scored a 15 in that same skill, they cannot necessarily be compared to each other. It does not necessarily mean that the other person is weaker than you in that particular skill. The strengths and weaknesses of you and another person can be compared, but not the absolute scores.

So your score of 18 must be viewed in relation to the other Executive Skills scores within your set of answers. So if 18 is your lowest score, that would be one of your lowest skills. The other person's 15 might be their lowest skill, or perhaps not, depending on their other scores. If by chance all of your scores are relatively high, which is possible, you should identify the lowest individual answers to specific questions. It is likely that the specific Executive Skills in which you have the lowest answers are, in fact, your weakest skills.

Once you know your strongest and weakest skills, you can focus on just those skills for much of the remainder of this book, since those will be the only skills needing attention. More likely, you will start to match certain characteristics of strengths and weakness to those around you. The next step is to analyze your combination of skills and determine how much effort is associated with tasks that play to your strengths and weaknesses, which we discuss in Chapter 2.

2

Combinations of Executive Skills and the Effortful Task

ONCE YOU UNDERSTAND your personal combinations of Executive Skills, you can tweak aspects of your current job and better plan future career moves and potentially new directions. With each skill there are certain characteristics or tendencies you can identify based on your highest and lowest Executive Skills. The combination of your strongest and weakest Executive Skills presents the most opportunity.

At the least, knowing your own combination also can show you how much work you will *feel* like you're doing when dealing with certain tasks. Although it might be obvious to you that certain things seem easier for some people and more difficult for others, until now you might not have understood why. It is because the strengths in a person's Executive Skills that best match those skills needed for a certain task can make that task feel more natural for that person to perform. So if a task requires certain skills that play to your Executive Skills strengths, the task takes less effort for you. Conversely, if the task requires certain skills that are among your weakest, then you will find that it takes considerably more effort. As a result, the same task that requires your strengths would take considerably more effort for someone who is low in the same Executive Skills.

An *effortful task* is one that requires skills that are your weakest Executive Skills. The task is still doable, but at a higher amount of effort and difficulty. It also is not the best positioning for you long term, as we discuss later, since you should be trying to play to your strengths in Executive Skills.

A task that is not an effortful task is one that plays to your Executive Skills strengths, making it easier for you to accomplish. For example, if you are high in Time Management, it is easier for you to remember to get to a meeting on time than it is for someone who is low in that skill. And if you are low in Working Memory, it is tougher for you to remember directions while driving on a business trip than for someone who is high in Working Memory, for whom it almost seems like second nature. It's not that the person can't get to a meeting on time, but it will take more effort for them to manage it. And if you are low in Working Memory, you still can find your way somewhere, it just takes more effort and concentration on your part. You may even find yourself turning off the radio so you can better concentrate on finding your way. It is an effortful task.

When you're under a lot of pressure at work or are fatigued for whatever reason, it will be the effortful task that will become significantly harder to do or will fall apart altogether. So if you're low in the Executive Skill of Self-Restraint, when under pressure you will tend to say things that you are likely to regret later. And if you are low in the skill of Task Initiation, you are likely to find yourself procrastinating in more tasks, even perhaps to the point of freezing the forward motion of anything of import. You might even get so frustrated that you decide to put off the task till tomorrow.

It's natural to gravitate to tasks that are not effortful or at least of lower effort, which explains why people drift to certain things at work and at home. Paying the bills on a regular schedule would be much easier for someone who is high in Organization, and starting a lengthy report would be easier for someone high in Task Initiation. Through childhood, as Executive Skills are fully developing, children tend to most use those skills that come easiest. This trend continues, so that by adulthood, when Executive Skills are fixed, the strongest skills tend to be those that have been exercised the most, essentially making them even greater strengths.

If you strive to get yourself into situations that leverage your strongest combinations of Executive Skills, you will have not only a higher chance of success, but the tasks you perform will be easier for you, since they will not be effortful tasks, which we discuss in more detail later in this chapter as well as in Chapter 3.

What Your Strengths Look Like

Since your Executive Skills strengths are unique, you can look at yours and see the behaviors that typically go with those skills. For example, if your highest skills are Emotion Control and Stress Tolerance, you would likely be able to get the job done, be unemotional and cool under pressure, able to resist temptations, resilient in the face of setbacks, not easily discouraged or sidetracked, able to maintain control in pressure situations, have a high tolerance for ambiguity, and be emotionally steady in a crisis. Following are the characteristics associated with Executive Skills strengths. Although you can identify your potential behaviors based on those skills, you also will start to notice the strengths of others. You can also now identify the likely traits behind some of their behaviors.

HIGH IN SELF-RESTRAINT

Characteristics: Informed decision making, methodical and deliberate approach, avoids impulsivity.

- You decide to delay commenting on your boss's new idea

- You tell a client you'll get her a price quote after you gather more information rather than just providing a price on the spot, which may be based on incomplete information

- Your teenage daughter calls for permission to stay out an extra two hours and you tell her you'll call her back after discussing it with your spouse

> **Scenario: The Self-Restrained Manager**
> Robert would never shoot his mouth off without thinking. When he was a teenager, he never got in trouble with teachers and never lost after-school jobs for telling his supervisor what was on his mind without thinking through the consequences. When entering the full-time workforce after graduating, this pattern continued. Robert naturally used space-filler comments to stall for time, something like "that's an interesting idea" or "I've never looked at it that way, let me give it some thought." He had a natural ability to bite his tongue, which saved him from difficult situations when he moved into management, both with his senior management and with those he supervised. The more he practiced this skill, the more he realized that taking his time gave him the opportunity to look at a situation from multiple perspectives and consider factors that didn't occur to him in the heat of the moment. Coworkers often said of him that if you were looking for someone to think something through and consider all the angles before giving you an answer, then Robert is the one to see.

HIGH IN WORKING MEMORY

Characteristics: The ability to do one task without losing sight of other commitments or obligations, reliable, can be counted on to follow through, able to keep eye on the ball.

- Instead of using a planner, you rely on personal memory and it works

- When you go shopping, you never need a list

- When your spouse asks you to do something when you're done with what you're doing now, you always remember to do it

> **Scenario: Remembering the Right Stuff**
> One of Nancy's strongest Executive Skills is Working Memory. She scored high in this skill because she has a remarkable ability to hold

complex information in her head and to remember the details she needs to keep track of in her role as a project leader for several major company initiatives. When she gets sidetracked by a phone call from her boss or a request to trouble-shoot an emergency, Nancy is able to return to the project at hand and pick up where she left off. But although Nancy's memory is strong, she has also developed strategies for improving her skills even more. She keeps her PDA handy with separate files for each of the major projects she's working on. As soon as a project is assigned and she and her team have developed a time line, she gets a team member who is weaker in Working Memory to establish a tickler system to keep him on track.

Nancy's husband is vice president of marketing at a Fortune 1000 company, and together they must manage a complicated schedule to make sure childcare is always available for their three children. Nancy always remembers her home obligations as well those at work. She blocks off time for her children's school and sports events to make sure she doesn't take on work obligations that conflict with family responsibilities. She easily created a system of coding her notations so that she knows which obligations are firm and which are flexible.

HIGH IN EMOTION CONTROL

Characteristics: Not easily sidetracked, gets the job done, unemotional/cool under pressure, has capacity to resist temptations, resilient in the face of setbacks, not easily discouraged.

- You do not get upset when things don't go as planned

- Your teenage son deliberately says something to "push your buttons" and you keep your cool

- When a coworker criticizes your work at a team meeting, you make a calm, reasoned response

Scenario: Obstacles Seen as Bumps in the Road

Philip is exceptionally good at mobilizing his energies to get work done. He can put a positive spin on almost any task that comes his way. While coworkers become bogged down by details or avoid the unpleasant aspects of work, Philip is able to find ways to attack them. This sometimes involves creating an image and setting his sights on the fun part of the work. Other times it means rehearsing difficult phone calls to reduce anxiety. When things don't go as planned, Philip thinks of obstacles as simple bumps in the road. When challenges cross his path, he sometimes thinks "Have to change a flat tire and then I'll be on my way again." When a colleague tries to deliberately thwart his work, Philip doesn't allow himself to become sidetracked by negative emotion, and he doesn't let office politics get in the way of doing his job.

HIGH IN FOCUS

Characteristics: Task focused, able to stay immersed in a task, able to screen out distractions.

- Even though tired, you can concentrate on an important proposal

- You pay attention to an important but personally uninteresting presentation

- When paying the bills, you can handle interruptions

- In a noisy office, you can still concentrate on a phone call

Scenario: Finishing a Project

Once Bill starts a project, no matter how big, he focuses his energy on seeing it through to completion. After much thought over a period of time, Bill and his wife agreed they would add a deck to their house. After picking up the appropriate wood and supplies, Bill started the project. When a neighbor dropped by to chat, Bill politely said he had to get back to work, but would be happy to get together after the deck was finished. When his wife suggested Bill join her shopping, he reminded her that they had agreed to build the deck and that he had to keep working to assure that it was completed when they agreed. When his wife suggested replacing the front porch light fixtures, Bill tells her exactly how much there is left to do on the deck and reminds her that he can be most efficient when he can finish one project before taking on another.

Bill has noticed that when he gets diverted from a task before it's completed, he feels a little anxious. The project seems to nag at the back of his mind until he can get back to it and see it through to the end. There are times that Bill finds his interest in a project lagging, and he knows that affects his energy level. When this happens, he takes a break and writes down the remaining tasks that need to be done. Sometimes Bill imagines a reward he can give himself once the project is done. It may be taking his wife out to dinner, or taking a day off to play golf. Having those things to look forward to keeps him going on the project.

HIGH IN TASK INITIATION

Characteristics: Gets the job started without delay, is action oriented.

- Given an assignment that is due in three weeks, you do it right away

- You start the ball rolling on a project before someone directs that it be started

- You write a check for a bill the day you receive it

> **Scenario: Starting Right Away**
> Joanne's favorite phrase is "There's no time like the present." She's found that she has much more energy for tasks when she can begin them right away. Even when her plate is full, Joanne makes an effort to at least begin a new undertaking shortly after it's assigned. When this isn't possible, she blocks off time in her schedule to start the new project. Because she's energized by starting new tasks, Joanne likes beginning something new near the end of the week because it gives her something to look forward to. When coworkers get stuck, they often turn to Joanne for help getting started on tasks, since she has a practical way of viewing things that make it easy to identify first steps.

HIGH IN PLANNING/PRIORITIZATION

Characteristics: Clear thinking, aptitude to develop step-by-step processes, able to differentiate what's important and what's not.

- You plan your vacation months ahead of time

- You always set priorities when you have a lot to do

- You are not easily overwhelmed by the big assignment

> **Scenario: Planning a Project**
> Jason has an exceptional ability to know what he wants a project to look like when it's completed and to work his way back to the beginning to map out a plan. He can easily see the prerequisites and all the things that need to be put in place before the project can be started. He can analyze each of the required tasks, both to identify them individually and to determine a sequence to follow that will make the entire project go smoothly. He also is adept at sorting out what kinds of tasks do not fit the project plan or selecting from an array of alternative approaches if necessary.

HIGH IN ORGANIZATION

Characteristics: Keeps track of belongings, inclined to be neat, pays attention to detail.

- You arrange your schedule to manage the week's work

- You pay your bills on a regular schedule

- You always keep your bedroom neat

- You always clean your e-mail in-box (you may also be high in Time Management)

- You can easily find a file that your manager needs for a meeting

> **Scenario: A Basket for Everything**
> Diane's name is synonymous with organization. It's not that her workspace is obsessively tidy, but just that she has a system for managing things so that what she needs is always at her fingertips. She has a series of baskets geared to the work at hand. One is for material that needs immediate response, a second is for material that needs a response within a week, and a third is for whenever there's

time. She handles her e-mail the same way, and everything that needs to get out that day, gets done. Diane has electronic file folders for every project she's working on, uniquely organized for her, with each sub-task listed under the appropriate file. Diane's file folders are color coded to make it easy to identify each project and reduce the likelihood of anything being misplaced.

Each Friday, Diane surveys her physical and electronic in-baskets and prepares for the next week. Sometimes her colleagues tease her about her organization methods and wonder if she organizes her home life the same way. She is embarrassed to tell them that she does, but she knows how much time it saves her, and it keeps the family running smoothly. She is considered the *go-to* person around the office

HIGH IN TIME MANAGEMENT

Characteristics: Efficient, able to meet deadlines, methodical.

- You are always on time for just about everything

- You arrive at a meeting on time despite heavy traffic

- You always clean your e-mail in-box

- When you ask someone to do something, you always want it done right away

Scenario: Spending Time Wisely

Greg could hire himself out as a time management expert. He uses a daily, weekly, and monthly planning system that allows him to use his time efficiently and stay on course. At the end of each day, Greg spends a few minutes planning how he'll spend his time the next day. He does the same thing at the end of the week, writing an outline of what he wants to accomplish the following week and blocking times for specific tasks.

Greg organizes his workday so that time doesn't get away from him. He answers e-mails twice a day, returns phone calls in early afternoon, and closes his door when he needs to work without interruptions. Greg knows how to say *no* and how to delegate. When he runs a meeting, Greg makes sure it has a tight agenda, and he sticks to it. He only attends those meetings where his presence is

> necessary, and in a polite but efficient way makes sure the meetings are focused on specific tasks and real outcomes.

HIGH IN DEFINING AND ACHIEVING GOALS

Characteristics: Able to achieve long-term goals, task-focused, can be relied upon for task completion.

- You always send in the rebate forms (you may also be high in Organization)

- Assigned to an extra project, you complete it as well as your current duties

- Even if momentarily distracted, you don't lose sight of the goal

- You always finish what you started

> **Scenario: Getting the Job Done**
> While some of the other managers tend to drop everything to go after the next hot idea, Ryan's pursuit of goals is always steady. When his supervisor has a long-term project that absolutely has to get done, he always knows to whom to turn, since Ryan always brings a project to completion. He is good at setting a goal and then is not distracted by short-term issues that come along, no matter how interesting they appear to those around him. Ryan always figures the best tactics to reach the goals, ranging from regular reporting from subordinates to meeting with his boss if she tries to divert staff or resources to other tasks or projects.

HIGH IN FLEXIBILITY

Characteristics: Independent, high tolerance for ambiguity, able to integrate new information, adaptable to change course.

- When the first solution to a problem doesn't work, you easily think of another solution

- You're great at seeing other people's perspectives in a problem situation

- You adjust easily to unexpected changes in plans or schedules

> **Scenario: Changing Gears Easily**
>
> Jonathan is known around the office as a problem solver, someone to whom to turn when plans hit a snag. He seems to have a remarkable ability to reframe bad news and find something positive in situations. When his team encounters a roadblock, Jonathan can be counted on to see his way around the obstacle. He once worked hard to set up training for his staff regarding a major new computer software system the company was implementing. The day before the scheduled training, Jonathan was informed that there were not enough training materials to go around. Jonathan very quickly decided to divide the group into teams of two and have them share materials, seeing the added benefit of having certain people work closely together. Jonathan immediately checked the list of participants to consider the best matches.

HIGH IN OBSERVATION

Characteristics: Able to observe one's own actions, self-reflective, strategic thinker, can observe group process, impartial, and can see beyond oneself.

- In a project at work, you observe how other team members approach things differently from you

- The boss makes a negative comment and you figure out how you will do better next time

- When conflicts arise between you and your spouse, you are easily able to see how your behavior contributed to the problem and decide to work to fix it for the next time around

> **Scenario: Working to Get Better**
>
> Stacey has always been able to evaluate herself and improve what she does as she goes. Whenever she faces a challenge, she deals with it but always looks back to see how she could have done it differently. For example, for years Stacey has taken responsibility for planning the details of the family vacation. Her husband and three children all gladly welcome this, since each trip seems to get better for them. After each vacation, Stacey mentally notes the best and worst parts with an eye toward improving the next one. She has

observed that on flights of more than three hours her children get antsy and sometimes crabby, and she remembers this when she and her husband plan their next vacation. Stacey's children greatly appreciate that their mother always asks them what they liked and disliked about the last vacation and seeks their advice on how to improve the next one.

HIGH IN STRESS TOLERANCE

Characteristics: Maintains control in pressure situations, emotionally steady in a crisis.

- You see unexpected obstacles as interesting challenges to be overcome

- You find yourself feeling bored or tired when your work follows a routine

- You enjoy taking on tasks that incorporate uncertainty or unpredictability

Scenario: Cool Under Pressure
Drew likes working under fire. Routines and predictability bore him, and he is energized by a crisis. Any sudden change of plans is just fine with him, because he enjoys the uncertainty and demand for on-the-feet thinking. Drew is the one getting on a plane, cellphone in hand, gathering last-minute information about a problem to be solved as he travels to the site of the problem. During the flight, Drew is hard at work on his computer drafting contingency plans. He can picture many different scenarios and imagines a response to each one. By the time Drew arrives at the crisis, he's already done the preliminary work. However, he finds things have changed again, with people in a panic. He calmly makes some minor adjustments to his solutions and moves forward plotting a course of action.

Task Effort

You and everyone around you at work will face both effortful and non-effortful tasks on a regular basis. Your objective should be to navigate into situations that play to your Executive Skills strengths, but there will be situations in which you must deal with both high- and low-effort tasks. The question is which you do first.

If you've been saving the effortful tasks for last, you're not alone. When it comes to tackling tasks, the majority of senior executives and managers also tend to save for last those tasks that take a high amount of effort (see Survey 2-1).

SURVEY 2-1: Task Effort
When it comes to tasks (that you are capable of doing) at work, how much effort does it take for those tasks that you tend to do first?

Extremely high amount	7%
Somewhat high amount	43%
Somewhat low amount	44%
Extremely low amount	6%

When it comes to tasks (that you are capable of doing) at work, how much effort does it take for those tasks that you tend to do last?

Extremely high amount	16%
Somewhat high amount	48%
Somewhat low amount	27%
Extremely low amount	8%

When it comes to tasks (that you are capable of doing) at work, how much effort does it take for those tasks that you tend to do first?

	Senior Executive	Manager
Extremely high amount	11%	2%
Somewhat high amount	39%	49%
Somewhat low amount	44%	44%
Extremely low amount	6%	5%

When it comes to tasks (that you are capable of doing) at work, how much effort does it take for those tasks that you tend to do last?

	Senior Executive	Manager
Extremely high amount	13%	19%
Somewhat high amount	64%	55%
Somewhat low amount	25%	30%
Extremely low amount	9%	7%

As you can see from the survey, more executives than managers tend to first do those tasks that take an extremely high amount of effort. "The higher you go, the more you do the hard stuff first," says Terry Sullivan, president of the Western Energy Institute, a regional and international trade association of energy companies. "It takes more discipline to get higher in an organization."

Interestingly, discipline itself is generally a combination of Executive Skills, based on the specific task being tackled. For example, someone moving up in an organization might appear to be highly disciplined because she starts tasks right away (high in Task Initiation), keeps cool under pressure (high in Emotion Control), and constantly keeps her eye on the ball (high in Focus).

VOICES FROM THE FRONT LINES
Task Effort

"In direct contrast to most management advice books, I find that attacking the easier tasks first creates a more efficient work day. Eliminating the small allows me to focus exclusively on the larger tasks, while delaying the small to focus on the large often means that the small tasks become large, thus creating a vicious circle."

■

"I have always felt it better, no matter what, to tackle some easy things early on. It's better to have some small successes early on to bolster confidence and energy for the longer haul issues."

■

"The challenge with starting and completing tasks is largely driven by the multitude of things that come across my desk or through my door. Like most people, I enjoy doing certain tasks and might lean towards those first. On the other hand, I find doing the most difficult

or least desirable stuff first gets it out of the way and can make the day feel better."

·

"Based on priorities first, I then clear the deck of easily resolved problems so I can concentrate on more complex tasks without so many distractions."

·

"You give the small (fast) things priority and you get lots of them out of the way so you can then turn to the larger (lengthier) tasks which naturally take more time."

·

"Too many tasks, too little time and staffing anymore. Drowning in a sea of trivial duties can be the death of an active manager."

·

"A lot depends on the amount of time it will take to complete the task. If I can squeeze in a high amount of effort/minimal time task between longer time tasks, I'll do it. Generally, because the high amount of effort tasks are more long-term, I may be working on them in stages. They would be completed after lower effort tasks but may have been started and in progress during many low-effort tasks."

Don't Save the Hardest for Last

In general, it is not a good idea to save the effortful tasks for last. It's fine to start with an easier task, as sort of a warm-up, but the effortful tasks take the most energy, so they should be tackled at the highest energy part of your day. If you have your highest energy in the morning, that is when you should tackle the effortful tasks. For those who are energized in say, early afternoon, that is where the effortful tasks should go. There obviously are extenuating circumstances over which you have no control, such as the time for your presentation being suddenly moved up or an unexpected directive from above. In these cases, it will not matter whether the task is high or low effort; you will have no choice but to deal with it. But at least you'll know under which category it falls, either effortful task or not, so that you can psychologically gear yourself accordingly. You'll know whether you should expect to expend a high or low degree of energy for the particular task based on how it matches against your Executive Skills strengths and weaknesses.

"I find that I perform best when I take on the higher tasks first," says Sullivan of the Western Energy Institute. "If I have, say, ten tasks, but one is significant and the others much smaller, I start with the most difficult or significant until I'm either done or tired by it. I then fill in time with the less strenuous tasks before returning to the big one when my energy is higher. This works particularly well for me being a morning person, as I can give my best energy to the hardest tasks."

For example, when the energy trade association that Sullivan heads was launching a course on business acumen, the biggest part of the project for Sullivan involved convening and facilitating the curriculum development team. "The hardest tasks, gathering materials and data and preparing them for discussions, were essential to having efficient meetings. With most of the team traveling from out of town to participate this was particularly important."

As in the case of Sullivan's meeting preparation, an effortful task for someone often is tied to actions or activities of others. So when the hardest tasks are put off until later, there can be domino consequences down the line. If you start with the effortful tasks and they also are perceived by others to be high effort as well, you can gain the added benefit of getting a reputation as the person to turn to when something difficult needs to get done.

Typical Combinations of Skills

There are certain combinations of Executive Skills that go naturally with each other, and there are some that conflict with others. For example, if you scored high in Time Management, Task Initiation, and Focus, you likely scored low in Flexibility, since being highly organized, efficient, and focused do not generally allow for a high degree of flexibility. This is often, but not always, the case. Combinations can be either strengths or weaknesses. Here are some common combinations.

■ *Working Memory and Focus.* If these are your highest strengths, you likely can heavily rely on your personal memory no matter how busy it gets. You don't have to rely on lists as much as others and things don't tend to fall through the cracks. You find that even when you're a bit tired you can still concentrate on an important task and can even pay attention to an important presentation, even if it doesn't interest you.

If you are low in both, you might forget something important unless you write it down and certainly would need lists to stay on track. You might tell someone you will do something later, but then it totally slips your mind. You might find yourself daydreaming when reading a lengthy report and can be easily sidetracked by conversations at the office that keep you from doing what you should be doing. You might find yourself thinking of something else while working and might get tired before finishing a project.

▪ *Observation and Defining/Achieving Goals.* If these are your two greatest strengths, you likely are self-reflective and can easily review your past actions while seeking ways to use that knowledge to do better in the future. You have a pretty good understanding of how you solve problems and can easily observe how other team members approach things differently than you. In a conflict situation, you can easily see how you might have contributed to the problem. You generally meet the goals you set for yourself and can keep your eye on the ball, even with distractions. You tend to finish the big project you started some time ago.

If you are low in both, you might not notice a group's reaction to your ideas or actions, whether positive or negative. You would likely perceive certain problems or issues as unsolvable, due to factors out of your control. You might not generally finish everything you start, and might set goals that are somewhat vague. These goals can be abandoned quickly in the face of obstacles. You tend to accept opportunities as they come along, even though they might get in the way of something already underway.

▪ *Planning/Prioritization and Observation.* If these are your highest, you likely are highly organized, quite efficient, and able to stay with the task at hand. You're good at making lists that define steps that lead to project completion. You can easily determine what is and what is not important and can handle a big assignment. In that big assignment, you're good at monitoring your own performance against the incremental steps as you go. You take criticism in a positive way, using it to figure how to do better.

If these are your two weakest skills, you likely have trouble hitting goals, especially those that are longer term. You might find yourself walking away from a well-thought-out project because a new idea or project intrigues you. Subordinates may continually interrupt you to ask what to do next. By day's end, you may have no plan on what precisely you will do the next day. When planning an approach to something, you easily consider the same tactics that previously failed on the same type of activity.

■ *Self-Restraint and Defining/Achieving Goals.* If these are your two strengths, you would consider something thoughtfully before commenting on it. You favor informed decision making, are methodical and deliberate in making decisions, especially those that are important. You're not impulsive and hold off on commenting on a superior's idea until you think about it. You are not likely to overcommit with customers, preferring to check back at the office first. You can stay focused on the current task and don't let obstacles get in your way. You're good at setting goals and sticking to them over time, no matter what happens along the way.

If these are your two lowest skills, you might find yourself frequently apologizing for saying something you didn't mean, because it just came out. You might find yourself in trouble with a client or customer because you promised a bit too much to close the deal and now can't deliver. You might respond too quickly to an e-mail before reading the entire message or considering the consequences of your reply to all. You also are probably more concerned with the present, getting excited by new ideas as they are presented, despite how full your plate already is. You're considered a great start-up person but not one to deal with lengthy and complex projects that may require a lot of internal diplomacy. This could explain why an entrepreneur might not be the best person to take the business forward once it begins to mature.

■ *Time Management, Task Initiation, and Focus.* If these three are your strengths, you would be good at meeting deadlines through your efficiency and methodical approaches to almost everything. You're good at figuring out how long it will take to complete complex projects. When you want something done, you usually want it done now. Starting a task right away and finishing it on time seem very natural to you and you appear to others to be an action-oriented person. Once you get started on something, you stick with it until completion. Your reputation for making deadlines is well recognized, and you easily screen out distractions to get done what you need to get done.

If these are your three lowest skills, you often find yourself in a last-minute crunch before a meeting or presentation. You might lose track of time on a very busy day, wondering how the day went by so fast and how so little got done. You're often late for meetings as well as for other things in life, and you tend to put off until tomorrow everything you can. You sometimes have to be reminded to do something and find very good reasons to put things off until later. While working, you easily think of things other than what you're working on and are easily sidetracked, often before a project is even started.

▪ *Emotion Control and Stress Tolerance.* If these are your two strengths, you remain calm when publicly criticized and don't get upset when the day doesn't go as planned. Your emotions don't usually get in the way of what you're working on and you are not easily sidetracked or discouraged. You are seen as being a person who is always cool under pressure, and you quickly bounce back after an emotional setback. You can work well under pressure and welcome huge challenges, which you handle with emotional calm.

If these are your two lowest skills, you can feel defensive about a negative comment about something you or your department did, and it could bother you for hours. You can feel badly if a meeting did not go as well as you had thought it might. When under pressure, you might seem irritable to others and at such times have a tough time keeping your anger in check. You're somewhat resistant to change and would be emotionally stressed in a crisis situation. You likely would feel more secure knowing your schedule for the next few weeks and get anxious if things around you start happening too quickly or not exactly as planned. You're likely to be very comfortable in a daily routine.

Common Opposites of Skills

Just as there are certain combinations of Executive Skills that naturally pair, there are skills that are opposites and naturally conflict with each other. In many cases, if one is your greatest strength, the opposite will be a weakness, and vice versa. Following are some typical opposites.

• *Flexibility vs. Time Management.* If you are high in Flexibility and low in Time Management, you are rather independent and tend to go with the flow. You can change directions easily and revise plans on a moment's notice. You also tend to lose track of time. The meetings you run don't usually start on time but they can take interesting and unexpected turns based on the discussions you allow to occur.

If you are low in Flexibility and high in Time Management, you would be a bit more efficient in your approach to everything and would tend to run on time, almost across the board. You would start the meeting on time, and have little patience for someone who tends to introduce irrelevant topics during that meeting.

• *Working Memory vs. Organization.* If your strength is Working Memory and weakness Organization, you likely are considered reliable and can be counted on to remember the important things. You're good with recalling names and dates when under pressure and recall almost exactly who agreed to do what at that meeting several weeks ago. You're prone to misplace or lose things at times and don't have a great system for storing information. The good news is that you recall the information even if you can't find where you put the document.

If you are weak in Working Memory and strong in Organization, you can't remember the information but you have a system so that you can easily find the document. You would likely write many things down to remember to do them. At times, you forget to do something you promised but once something is written on your regular schedule, it occurs. Although Working Memory and Organization are common opposites, there are some people who can have them both as strengths or both as weaknesses.

• *Stress Tolerance vs. Time Management.* If you are strong in Stress Tolerance and weak in Time Management, you tend to thrive in stressful situations and are comfortable with uncertainty and change. You can handle deadlines being moved and even welcome the challenge of working through the night to finish a major task. You might even end up working through the night to finish that task because you underestimated how long it would take. You can handle stress, which is sometimes caused by your own inefficiency.

If you are weak in Stress Tolerance and strong in Time Management, you would tend to be hesitant to change schedules and might become emotionally stressed in a crisis situation. However, you would be efficient and tend to make deadlines. You would be punctual and on task, but could get rattled by anyone diverting you from what you are working on.

▪ *Task Initiation vs. Flexibility.* If you are high in Task Initiation and low in Flexibility, you tend to start things as soon as they are assigned and then are relatively stubborn about changing once in motion. You hit the ground running, but you also find yourself more comfortable with rules and directives from others. Once you start, you don't want to be interrupted, even if it is to receive new and relevant information.

If you are low in Task Initiation and high in Flexibility, you tend to procrastinate and come up with any reason not to start on the next project or task. You are very comfortable working independently, though things take longer than expected due to the lag before starting.

▪ *Self-Restraint vs. Flexibility.* If you are strong in Self-Restraint and weak in Flexibility, you take time to consider your comments and prefer informed decision making. You internally decide on a course of action and then tend to stick with it to the point of becoming unnerved when someone wants to change it.

If you are weak in Self-Restraint and strong in Flexibility, you are first to speak your mind, often saying too much too soon, before thinking it through. You are independent and like changing course, though you might tend to make a negative, off-the-cuff remark when you do change.

Situations That Play to Certain Combinations of Executive Skills

Another way to look at combinations of skills is by what types of job characteristics match which types of skills. These are situations that would be best done by someone with particular strengths in certain Executive Skills. Here are some common combinations matched against certain job functions or job activities with which Executive Skills strengths would be most suitable.

■ *Detail Work.* Any task or job that requires a lot of fine detail, such as constantly tracking disparate pieces of information, would best be done by someone who is high in the skills of Organization and Working Memory.

■ *Strategy.* An activity or position that requires creative or out-of-the box thinking would in general best be done by someone high in the skills of Observation and Flexibility.

■ *Troubleshooting, Crisis Management.* An activity that requires dealing with constant turmoil and/or high pressure would be best suited for someone high in the skills of Stress Tolerance, Flexibility, and Emotion Control.

■ *Working Alone.* If you are considering a work situation that requires you to work alone much of the time, such as working out of a home office, your high Executive Skills should be Task Initiation, Focus, and Time Management. Otherwise, you might find yourself spending much of your time drifting through the day without getting much accomplished.

■ *Highly Interactive.* Work situations that require a high degree of interactions with many people would require the Executive Skill of Flexibility. Two examples would be a position where there is a lot of teamwork that requires participation, such as being a manager or member of a project team, or situations that require dealing with many people within short spans of time, such as a call center manager.

Working Against Type

It is possible to be involved in such tasks even though you do not have the particular required Executive Skills strengths, but you would be doing what is called *working against type.* Basically, it is not a good fit. You *can* do certain types of jobs if they require your weakest skills, but it will be an effortful task. In addition, when you're under pressure, your weaknesses will become very obvious, if not to you, then certainly to those around you. For example, if you were in a troubleshooting role and were low in the skill of Emotion Control, you would be likely to lose your cool when under the gun, perhaps prompting an outburst that you might have controlled in a calm situation. However, if you were high in the Skills of Observation and Flexibility, working on long-range planning with a diverse group, for example, would not be an effortful task for you. It also would be a situation in which you would likely make positive contributions of ideas. The best approach is to play to your strengths, which we discuss in detail in Chapter 3.

3

Learning to Play
to Your Strengths

SINCE EXECUTIVE SKILLS are relatively unchangeable, the greatest opportunity is to leverage those that are your strongest. Despite what might be stated, common practice in many businesses is that people should work to improve their weaknesses or shortcomings. Just the opposite should be done. Once you identify your strongest inherent Executive Skills, you can and should capitalize on those strengths, while supplementing or working around those that are your greatest weaknesses, which we detail in Chapter 4.

Now that you know your strongest and weakest Executive Skills, you might better understand why you do well in some situations and not in others. One reason could be that your boss, department, or organization is not playing to your strengths. Through no fault of yours or your employer, you might find yourself in a position that just doesn't suit what you're good at, and you and the boss might instinctively know it.

Executives and managers agree that their companies are not great at tapping into the greatest strengths of the people who work there. It is not that businesses are *bad* at utilizing the strengths of the people who work there, but that they are not *great* at it, when they could be. It's not as if companies don't try, as we discuss later, but much of the opportunity to get your organization to play to your strengths is in your hands.

Business leaders already think that their organizations are not great at tapping into the strengths of their executives or managers. Almost three-fourths of executives and managers feel their department or organization does not use what they consider to be their greatest strengths extremely well (see Survey 3-1 below).

With so many demands placed on each employee, it wouldn't be unusual for you to be called on to do something that's not remotely close to your Executive Skills strengths. "The organization does not look at what people do well," says one survey respondent. "They more or less dictate what they think you should do well because of their perception of your job. For example, a network administrator was told that he should program and implement a database, because it has to do with computers."

Says another: "Because of all the cutbacks, employees, myself included, have to pick up extra duties that are time-consuming, yet must be done. Time devoted to tasks that were once completed by another employee is not time and talent well spent."

This can help explain why you or others you know feel that the company is not taking advantage of what you or they have to offer. It can be because the company has no concrete idea of what your strongest and weakest Executive Skills are, or it could be that those particular skills are not needed for the specific job or task that you are charged with. The gap in perfectly matching your Executive Skills strengths to the job at hand also could explain why some tasks are easier or more natural for you while others are more difficult or challenging.

SURVEY 3-1: Tapping into Greatest Strengths
In general, how well does your department and/or organization tap into the greatest strengths of the people who work there?

Extremely well	22%
Somewhat well	61%
Not very well	15%
Not at all well	2%

In general, in your current position, how well does your department and/ or organization use what you consider to be your greatest strengths?

Extremely well	28%
Somewhat well	55%
Not very well	14%
Not at all well	4%

In general, how well does your department and/or organization tap into the greatest strengths of the people who work there?

	Small	Medium	Large
Extremely well	29%	13%	17%
Somewhat well	60%	65%	59%
Not very well	10%	18%	24%
Not at all well	1%	4%	0%

In general, in your current position, how well does your department and/ or organization use what you consider to be your greatest strengths?

	Small	Medium	Large
Extremely well	32%	25%	21%
Somewhat well	54%	54%	55%
Not very well	12%	15%	21%
Not at all well	2%	6%	3%

As you can see from the survey, smaller companies are somewhat better at tapping into the strengths of the people who work there. However, even if you work at a small company, it is likely that only about a third of departments or organizations are extremely good at tapping into your greatest strengths. And if you work at a large company, that number is only about a fifth. By learning to identify and play to your Executive Skills strengths, we believe the number of departments and entire organizations that play to your greatest strengths will increase as more of you become better at matching yourself to what you do.

> **Tapping into Greatest Strengths**
>
> *"Working with a very small staff, our main issue in this area is the amount of time and stress involved in doing things that are necessary, but are not core competencies for an individual. Too often the strengths of a particular person are underutilized because of the responsibilities that fall outside of their giftedness."*
>
> ■
>
> *"We have hired executive coaches and are going through a whole process review of our entire organization. So we are dealing with the negatives."*
>
> ■
>
> *"In my experience, it is the rare company that actively focuses on fully utilizing the strengths of its employees. They hire based on talent but they do not necessarily look to maximize all the talents and strengths of their employees. Too often we settle for getting the job done, and do not capitalize on the strengths of our employees."*

If you work in a small company, it's more likely that your department or organization is better at tapping into the strengths of those who work there. And if you are a manager at a small company, there is a better chance that your organization is tapping into what you have considered to be your greatest strengths. However, no matter the company size, there still is great room for improvement.

Executive Skills Capacity: Trapped by Success

The first step in dealing with tasks or events that you know in advance will be effortful for you is to identify them. If you find a certain task easy or enjoyable, chances are it plays to your Executive Skill strengths. If you dread the task and would rather do almost anything else, it probably plays to your weaknesses.

You can do an effortful task, but it is a better use of your time and resources to find someone else to do it for whom it is not an effortful task. For example, if you are low in Focus, then writing a report in a noisy office will be an effortful task for you. If you are also low in organization, writing a report in a quiet office would still be an effortful task for you. Better to get someone else in the office to write the report, or consider that it will take more effort every time you do it, since it is clearly a nonpreferred task. When you can't avoid doing effortful tasks, you may find that alternating between easy and effortful tasks makes them more bearable.

If, for whatever reasons, you have no choice but to do the task, then you should be aware that if you perform the task you might be stuck with it, whatever it is. At times, you might find yourself performing a task fairly well, even though it is an effortful task. For example, if you're the manager who is low in Focus and Organization but for the past year you've been writing the regular reports, it's a tough argument to make that someone else should now take over the responsibility. It could be that no one knows how difficult it has been for you to write those reports. If not careful, you can get trapped by success at an activity that is an effortful task. When the job at hand requires you to use one of your weakest skills, you can expend a high level of energy while using that particular Executive Skill.

This can affect entire careers. For example, if you have a job that requires that you regularly use a skill that is among your weakest, you might adapt either by working around your weakness or tweaking it just enough to get by. If a larger company is searching to fill a position requiring such a skill, you could end up being selected because you held a position where such a skill was required. If that career trend continues, it is very likely that sooner or later you will fail in that area as pressure on your weakest skills increases with the magnitude of the jobs requiring that skill. The key solution is to get yourself out of that situation.

There are cases, however, where it might be in your best interest to get into a temporary or transition situation that plays to your weaknesses. It could be that you clearly see that the next step or promotion after that temporary position plays to your strength. In this case, you will have to minimize the impact of your weakness until you get that promotion, which we discuss in Chapter 4.

Goodness of Fit

How well your Executive Skills strengths match a job or task is what we call *goodness of fit*. It is the alignment of your Executive Skills with your task or job. You can and should continually monitor your goodness of fit, because it can easily change over time, as the job you're in evolves, which we discuss in detail in Chapter 6.

To determine your goodness of fit requires you to analyze how your top two or three strengths and two or three weaknesses match the job. You can use the same benchmark to measure what is most needed in a particular job and then compare whether what is needed plays to your strengths. (See Questionnaire 3-1: Task Skills Required for a Job or Task, below.)

If you already are doing the job, this should be relatively straightforward. For example, you may already be aware that the job requires high Time Management, a skill in which you know you are low because you are continually being reprimanded for being late. The converse also could be the case, where you are high in Time Management and always find yourself on time, while everyone around you is always late, and no one seems to care.

Knowing and leveraging situations that play to your strengths can assure that there is always a goodness of fit for you. You also now can be aware that in a rare case, a manager can unwittingly (or for the cynically minded, wittingly) place you in a role that critically requires your three weakest Executive Skills to succeed. It is no secret that in some companies, people have been transferred to positions it appears they will hate, in hopes they will leave the company, thus allowing the manager to avoid the often arduous termination procedures.

A devious manager who is aware of Executive Skills could attempt to do this with precision, except you are now armed with this information. The irony is that a manager trying to reassign you to what he perceives as an undesirable position for you could end up, unwittingly, reassigning you to a position that plays to your greatest strengths. Your new job would now be easier for you because there will be fewer effortful tasks.

In such situations, anyone you deal with who is not aware of the knowledge of Executive Skills strengths and weaknesses you now possess will be disadvantaged. You will be able to readily identify and understand the reasons behind the behaviors of people in situations that you can accurately forecast as winning or losing propositions. You then can try to be either heavily involved in winning situations or attempt to pry yourself out of those destined to failure.

Ranking Executive Skills

Here is a way to rank which Executive Skills are needed for a job, task, or project. Be precise about what task you are measuring. For example, you can benchmark your entire job, or simply one aspect of it, such as your role in a project on which you are a team member. In the space below, describe the specific job or task:

_____

_____

How much of each of the following skills does the task or job listed above require? Use the following assessment to rank which Executive Skills are required for the particular job.

QUESTIONNAIRE 3-1: Task Skills Required for a Job or Task

Place a check mark next to the three executive skills most important to the job or task you identified above. These three skills then become the critical Task Skills needed for that particular job or task

Self-Restraint _____

This is the ability to think before you act. It is the ability to resist the urge to say or do something to allow the time to evaluate the situation and how a behavior might affect it.

Working Memory _____

This is the ability to hold information in memory while performing complex tasks and involves drawing on past learning or experience to apply to the situation at hand or to project into the future.

Emotion Control _____

This is the ability to manage emotions in order to achieve goals, complete tasks, or control and direct behavior.

Focus _____
> This is the capacity to maintain attention to a situation or task in spite of distractions, fatigue, or boredom.

Task Initiation _____
> This is the ability to begin projects or tasks without undue procrastination.

Planning/Prioritization _____
> This is the capacity to develop a road map to arrive at a destination or goal, knowing which are the most important signposts along the way.

Organization _____
> This is the ability to arrange or place according to a system.

Time Management _____
> This is the capacity to estimate how much time one has, to allocate it effectively, and to stay within time limits and deadlines. It involves a sense that time is important.

Defining and Achieving Goals _____
> This is the capacity to have a goal, follow through to the completion of the goal, and not be put off or distracted by competing interests.

Flexibility _____
> This is the ability to revise plans in the face of obstacles, setbacks, new information, or mistakes. It relates to adaptability to changing conditions.

Observation _____
> This is the capacity to stand back and take a birds-eye view of yourself in a situation and to be able to understand and make changes in the ways that you solve problems.

Stress Tolerance _____
> This is the ability to thrive in stressful situations and to cope with uncertainty, change, and performance demands.

Task Skills Required Compared to Your Executive Skills

In Questionnaire 3-1 (Task Skills Required for a Job or Task) above you identified the three highest-ranked skills required for the particular job or task. In the following worksheet, opposite the appropriate skills listed in the left column, enter a check mark of those three highest-ranked Task Skills. Then, in the right column, enter a check mark next to *your* three highest level Executive Skills, according to your answers to the self-assessment questions in Chapter 1. This should give you a good idea of how well you are matched for the particular job or task.

Task Skills vs. Your Executive Skills

	Task Skills Score	Your Executive Skills Score
Self-Restraint	_____	_____
Working Memory	_____	_____
Emotion Control	_____	_____
Focus	_____	_____
Task Initiation	_____	_____
Planning/Prioritization	_____	_____
Organization	_____	_____
Time Management	_____	_____
Defining/Achieving Goals	_____	_____
Flexibility	_____	_____
Observation	_____	_____
Stress Tolerance	_____	_____

Assessing Project Team Fit

Being part of the right mix on a team will be easier once you know your Executive Skills strengths. For example, if you're high in the skill of Observation and Flexibility, you most likely will be a great contributor in brainstorming sessions. If you're great in Time Management and Organization, you will likely feel comfortable and be proficient at preparing for and/or running the meetings.

When either joining or being named to a team for a particular project or task, try to get yourself into a role that matches your strengths. At the same time, avoid any roles that highlight your particular weaknesses. For example, if you're low in Task Initiation, avoid being put into the position of creating the meeting agendas. That would be an effortful task for you.

Keep in mind that you don't always have a choice as to what team you're on, and you may be placed on a team based on criteria other than Executive Skills strengths. For example, your boss might not be aware of Executive Skills and simply place you on a team based on how much you might learn by being on that team. According to Colm McLoughlin, managing director of Dubai Duty Free at Dubai International Airport:

"Selecting employees for a team, be it for a project, operations, or even an ad-hoc purpose, is a great opportunity to help the lateral development of employees. Employees, both managers and staff, must be very interested in all parts of our business and not just in their line function, and participating in such teams gives them that exposure and insight to other areas of the business. This lateral development is an important part of an employee's career development within our organization, and equally, the business benefits from such lateral interaction."

Like McLoughlin at Dubai Duty Free, your manager might be interested in having you gain experience outside of your immediate area of expertise to provide future benefit to the organization.

When being asked to join a team, take into consideration the overall benefits in addition to how well your Executive Skills match your proposed role in the group. You also can try to make sure that your Executive Skills strengths are taken into account along with the other team selection criteria.

There are other factors that your manager might use to place you on a team. For example, in the case of Dubai Duty Free, McLoughlin considers:

- Individual competence and knowledge of the particular area of the team's involvement.

- Interpersonal skills, specifically the ability to work well with peers.

- Current workload and the capacity to take on further tasks as a team member.

- Level of performance in the current position.

- Motivation level and whether the employee is trapped in a cycle of low motivation and low performance.

- Career development plans, and whether this team will help the employee develop the necessary skills.

This is but one example of the basis on which a manager may select team members, before being well versed in your Executive Skills strengths. If your manager uses several other reasons (such as those mentioned by McLoughlin above) to place you on a team, you should work to make Executive Skills an added part of the mix. Bring to your manager's attention your particular Executive Skills strengths and explain how you could play to these strengths to make the team more effective. You also should mention that you might be energized and motivated within a team that is tapping into your strengths, because most managers are on the lookout for anything that might further motivate subordinates.

As a retailer, Dubai Duty Free has a large number of front-line and support staff, with a relatively lean management team that runs the business. "Being part of a team is a good opportunity to motivate the many front-line and support employees who may not have had frequent promotions or other formal career progression opportunities and yet are extremely productive and valuable employees," says McLoughlin. "Teams are also a good way to energize employees and get them out of a cycle of low motivation and performance, and a much better way of dealing with them than asking them to resign."

So if you're being considered for a team, check how your Executive Skills strengths can not only be leveraged, but even exercised more significantly. The person selecting you or running the team may also be looking at your future role, such as in the case of Dubai Duty Free. "I try to ascertain if being on the team will help the person further develop the skills that he needs to increase his contribution to our company in the future," says McLoughlin. "As a CEO, it is necessary for me to have a vision of where a person may be within the organization a year or few years from now, and then use such opportunities to help them get closer to the vision. This is especially the case with middle and senior executives."

Your manager may also be juggling many factors when considering whether you should be on a particular team, such as those considered by McLoughlin at Dubai Duty Free:

"The biggest challenge in selecting who should be on a team is in juggling all of the factors and being seen to be fair in the selection. In selecting a team, as much as it would motivate an employee and benefit the business, it is equally important not to de-motivate those who did not get selected at that particular time. Another challenge is making sure that line managers, who may not be a part of the team in many cases, support the selection and participation of their staff in the team."

When joining a team, a quick assessment of the strengths of the other team members could serve you well. Keep in mind that some of them probably were selected specifically for some of the same reasons that McLoughlin uses, which may not include consideration of Executive Skills strengths and weaknesses. If the combinations of team members are way out of whack, there's a good chance that the mission of the team will not be accomplished.

For example, if a group, team, or task force is charged with developing a new product, it should contain a mix of Executive Skills strengths to assure success. If the group is loaded with people whose greatest strengths are Observation and Flexibility, the group is likely to come up with some great ideas, but without any emphasis on execution or how realistic or practical the ideas are to implement. On the other hand, if the team is loaded with people strong in Time Management, Organization, and Task Initiation, it will most likely devise the most executable plan, though the idea may be very weak. The key is to be involved in teams or groups that are well balanced, to ensure that the strengths of the participants are properly utilized.

If you're selected for a group or team, we suggest that you quickly assess the combination of Executive Skills strengths on the team before you end up wasting a lot of your precious time on something that could be destined for failure. If the team seems like it has a good combination of strengths, then quickly volunteer to fill a role that plays to your own strengths. Once you're on the team, Executive Skills dynamics can easily come into play.

Assessing Management Team Fit

The management team of an organization has a lot to do with whether the business succeeds or fails, and to what degree. You may be part of a great management team, or you may just be a keen observer of the management team in your organization. You might take delight in the foibles of a competitor's management team. You might think your organization has some weak spots in its management team, or you may perceive most of the players being all-stars. No matter the perspective, Executive Skills knowledge can provide you with new insight into the inner workings of a management team, as well as with possible reasons why they are dysfunctional.

You probably know of someone who either has risen through the ranks or come from the outside and who instantly seemed to fit within the management team. You might even be such a person. This could be because the person's Executive Skills strengths and weaknesses were a perfect fit with those immediately surrounding that executive.

Someone perfectly fitting into a management team could happen by accident, but more likely it will be through a rigorous interview and hiring process that indicates that the person is the correct one for a particular management spot. Though not all such moves ultimately work out, there are times when it seems the stars are aligned and the management team just clicks as a team. This could be because of great leadership, because business is on the upswing, because the team members may have many common interests, or any combination of things. The management team also could be a strong entity because of a great balance of Executive Skills strengths and weaknesses.

If several members of the management team are very strong in Observation, Planning/Prioritization, and Defining and Achieving Goals, the team is likely driven toward objectives and willing and able to take suggestions for improvement along the way. Issues such as Time Management and Working Memory may be handled by other managers strongest in those skills. Some of the activities related to those Executive

Skills may have been delegated to others, allowing each member of the management team to play to his or her strengths.

When Strengths Meet Strengths

People with certain Executive Skills strengths tend to get along with others of similar strengths, which only seems natural. For example, if your strongest skills are Time Management, Task Initiation, and Focus, you would tend to get along well with someone with the same strengths. You both would be deadline-driven, be inclined to start things right away, and be able to stay with the task until it's done. However, there are two downsides to always pairing with this kind of person in a project or task situation.

First, when you both have the same strengths, it is easy to ignore your weaknesses, since neither of you would be concentrating on them. When you both are strong in Time Management, Task Initiation, and Focus, you are likely both weak in Flexibility. This could create a situation where new, relevant, and perhaps important information is ignored for the sake of getting the task done on time. Once started, the two of you could be like a speeding train, staying exactly on the track you both perceived at the beginning to be the right track to the right place. No doubt you would arrive on time, but it may be at the wrong location based on new, but ignored, information.

Second, when both of you have the same strengths, you can easily become competitors. Whereas not in itself bad, competing on the same task or project can become detrimental to the outcome. With one of you trying to get something done faster than the other, there is increased room for error. There also is the potential to lose sight of the objective.

When Strengths Meet Weaknesses

Now that you know your strengths, you may find yourself more precisely identifying the strengths and weaknesses in those around you, such as coworkers, your boss, subordinates, and even your friends. This is only natural. You also might be able to recall an incident from the past when you wondered how a particular person you know could be so bad at something you find so easy or obvious. Now you know that the person's weakest Executive Skills probably were your strongest.

For example, if one of your strengths is Self-Restraint, it may absolutely baffle you how one of your colleagues can so often say such inappropriate things at the wrong time. Or if you're high in Time Management and Focus, it probably drives you crazy to see a certain person always be late for meetings for which you always arrive on time. What's even worse, if Time Management is the weakest skill of some senior executives or managers at an organization, meetings may always start and run late. Some businesses may refer to it as "company name here" time. So you might hear someone say, "Oh, we run on X time here," meaning we always run late. Although those executives or managers may find that company trait to be quaint, those high in Time Management may find it infuriating, even if they don't speak up. (For example, 85 percent of managers and executives say business would be better if more people would respect other people's time.) It is normal that you might not have thought of your strengths in this context, or not even thought of them at all.

It's common for a person with certain strengths to become frustrated with someone with corresponding weaknesses. This is especially true if your top two or three strengths are the other person's two or three greatest weaknesses. When you're very good at something, it can be unfathomable that others aren't as well. This can cause tension and conflict, mainly because of your frustration that the other person can perform so poorly at something that seems to you so easy.

The other person also can become frustrated, not understanding why you would be coming down on them for just being a little late for a meeting. They may be totally oblivious to their Executive Skills weaknesses or to how others see them. If they are low in Time Management, it might not cross their mind that being on time for meetings is all that important. Besides, in their world, they often lose sight of time, giving them what is (to them) a totally acceptable reason every time they are late.

If you have certain strengths and are working closely with a colleague with corresponding weaknesses, awareness helps a lot. Just *knowing* the corresponding Executive Skills in yourself and the other person can defuse a potential conflict. Without this knowledge, you could have become frustrated that your colleague couldn't accomplish what you consider simple activities, such as planning the day or getting started on projects on time, if those are among your strengths. The person with the weakness could become frustrated for being criticized or even teased for always being late, or being inflexible to change, for example. However, once you understand your strengths and weaknesses, you can connect with a colleague with opposite strengths and weaknesses and begin to complement each other.

If you're strong in Time Management and Task Initiation you are likely weak in Flexibility and Stress Tolerance. A colleague might be weak in your strengths, but strong in Flexibility and Stress Tolerance. You could agree that you'll work to make sure the other person gets to meetings on time, and agree to prod them to start activities they likely would put off. You get the other person to agree to help you keep your cool under pressure as well as ensure that you don't become too inflexible and unaware of what's going on around you when absorbed in a task. You might encourage the other person to force you to take a break, and periodically review where you are on a project to see whether the direction should be changed. The two of you working on a team could be a great combination, if each of you is allowed to play to your strengths while you manage each other's weaknesses.

Probably the most critical issue for you is to be aware of how your weaknesses may appear to others, especially your boss. If your Executive Skills weaknesses match his strengths, he may not comprehend why you're not acting how he thinks you should act, based on his strengths, of course.

If your boss is not aware of Executive Skills strengths and weaknesses, he could view your weaknesses as a motivational issue. When that happens, just keep in mind how difficult it is for you when your strengths are pitted against a coworker's weaknesses, and how frustrated you may have become. Your boss can be in the same situation. A person's Executive Skills greatest weaknesses often create what we call *blind spots,* so that the person with the weaknesses is unaware of how they look to a person who has those skills as strengths. We outline specific ways to deal with weaknesses in any Executive Skills in Chapter 4.

Executive Skills and Meetings

You probably can remember a series of meetings where attendees talked about the same thing for months, without ever taking any conclusive action. Suggestion after suggestion is brought up, with the discussion meandering all over the place. Or you might recall a time when someone hijacked a meeting, going on and on about a pet issue. Or you may remember that meeting where a few people kept bringing up new but totally unrelated issues, never allowing the meeting to stay on track. These all can be related to Executive Skills weaknesses. It could be a case of the team leader having the wrong set of Executive Skills to effectively lead the meeting, or of too many members being low in either Focus or Self-Restraint, allowing topics to drift.With your Executive Skills knowledge, you can likely now identify the specific problem areas of meetings you attend. A significant factor for meeting success lies with the Executive Skills profile of the person who is charged with the meeting's outcome. You know that a person strong in Time Management will start the meeting on time and keep it moving efficiently. You also can tell in advance how a meeting will be driven based on the agenda, whether they involve sharing of information, such as direct reports gathering with top management on a regular basis, or are aimed at specific outcomes.

You can observe meeting attendees and can identify what we call the *outliers*, those who never seem to participate, though they attend. The outliers could possibly be bored because they find the meeting irrelevant to them. On the other hand, they could be low in Focus, and could be thinking of something else, having lost interest early on. They might be low in Flexibility, and feel that other participants are speaking a different language. For example, at an off-site meeting to brainstorm new business development, you might notice a person from Finance not highly engaged. The person could be very strong in Organization and Time Management and low in Observation, not a natural combination to contribute to a new ideas session.

If you are that finance person and you're attending such a creative session, you can contribute, but only within your specific area of expertise. You can look at new ideas through the prism of your strengths. Since you would naturally gravitate toward efficiency, you might tackle the issue by considering ways to execute better, which might improve business at least as much as a new, untried idea.

If you are called to a meeting with your boss and you know she is low in Flexibility, it will not be a good idea for you to spring new things at that meeting and expect a positive response. The way to get around this is to send her the ideas in advance. If you will be presenting such ideas at a scheduled meeting, make sure anyone low in Flexibility has had a chance to consider the idea in advance, which will dramatically increase your chances of a positive reaction. When dealing with a boss whose strengths and weaknesses are very different from yours, it is best to be direct. For example, if you have a finance role and your boss is a highly creative type, you may want to preface your comments by saying something like, "We have different ways of looking at the world. My world is a world of numbers, so I'm not likely to be as creative as you." (You can skip the comment that you also know that she would have no chance of running a department as efficiently as you do.) Besides giving the boss a compliment, you have then set expectations that you might need time to ponder whatever the person is about to discuss and come at the issue somewhat differently.

Interviewing for the Perfect Fit Job

Since you know your Executive Skills strengths, you may have the opportunity to find the job that plays to those strengths. Part of playing to those strengths involves navigating yourself into positions that provide goodness of fit in the first place. This is important when considering a promotion or applying for a new job or position. When considering a new position, you should determine whether it requires high or low use of your top Executive Skills strengths. You can do this by probing during the interview process. For example, if your top strengths are Observation and Defining and Achieving Goals, you should ask questions regarding use of those particular skills in the job. You might ask how much the job requires analyzing problems, because this would be a characteristic of someone high in Observation. You might probe the importance of starting or running many tasks simultaneously or how deadlines are viewed within the organization, both characteristics of Defining and Achieving Goals. You may ask whether smaller tasks tend to be done serially, or several at a time—characteristics of Flexibility.

You also can ask questions to determine whether your Executive Skills weaknesses might be a problem. If you are low in Stress Tolerance, ask whether the business is very-deadline driven. If yes, being low in Stress Tolerance would not be a good fit. If the position has a degree of flexibility built in, as workload fluctuates, it might be a better fit. You can also ask whether the managers and employees at the business seem stressed at all, since most executives and managers today have a sense of stress in others around them, as well as in themselves.

If your lowest skill is Time Management, ask whether meetings in the organization typically start and run on time. If you are told that the organization prides itself on starting every meeting on time, you should probe deeper to see if it's just meetings or if the company culture is to run like a Swiss watch. If it is, you are likely to be walking into problems for yourself. You then will know if the job will require a low, medium, or high amount of Time Management. If you are low in Flexibility and the tasks are simultaneous and come fast and furiously, it is probably not a good fit.

A general way to think about the approach is to say to yourself, "These are my strengths," and then ask questions that would tell you whether the job in question would play to those strengths. If it does, then you should provide some examples from your past work experience that show how you have used those strengths in other situations, implying that you would use them well in the position under discussion. You should have these in mind before the interview and they should be easy to come up with, presuming you have been using some of your strengths at work.

Before accepting the position, you may also want to determine whether the person you will be working for has the same strengths and weaknesses as you, since they will become obvious to you once you start work in the new role. Just as you can ask questions about the job and the company, you can ask the same kinds of questions about the person for whom you would work, often the person interviewing you. By finding out their apparent strengths and weaknesses, you can immediately sense how you might work together. If your strengths match, you are likely to get along, but you may not be what the company really needs, though the interviewer may not know it.

When interviewing for a new position, keep in mind that if the person interviewing you has the same Executive Skills strengths as yours, he or she might feel you are the perfect candidate for the job. If that person is unaware of Executive Skills, you should carefully consider whether a job with matching strengths to that person would be best for you. The biggest consideration should be how well the job itself requires your strongest skills. So although the person doing the hiring may *like* you the best of all the candidates, it may be because of the perfect fit of your Executive Skills. But that does not necessarily mean you are a perfect fit for the job, which can be determined only by comparing your strengths with those required for the job.

In addition to using this approach while interviewing for a new job, it also can be used to start a discussion with your boss about your current position. You might have some thoughts on how to better play to your strengths, now that you know more precisely what they are based on. Once made aware of your Executive Skills strengths, your boss may know of some other areas to leverage those strengths. In advance, you should have examples of how you have used those strengths to help the business in the past.

Executive Skills at Home or Work

When you answered the questions in Chapter 1 you might have found yourself realizing that you sometimes behave differently at work from how you act at home, which is very natural. This doesn't mean your Executive Skill strengths and weaknesses are different in different locations; they are not. However, external elements can influence how you're required to behave in any given setting.

You could be high in a particular Executive Skill but find yourself not having to practice it in certain situations. For instance, you might be high in Working Memory but not always use that strength at home because your spouse is very high in the same Executive Skill. When you are together you might have little need to exercise your strength in family matters because your spouse so easily remembers the details to handle them.

You might be high in the skill of Observation but at the office you're part of a department that's totally operationally focused, not requiring that you even minimally use your strength in this arena. However, you might use that skill more at home, where you continually look at how you're raising your children and seek to improve. Your strengths and weaknesses are the same, but they're used differently in the different settings due to external factors.

ONE SKILL DIFFERENT AT HOME AND WORK: TASK INITIATION

We find that when it comes to the skill of Task Initiation, senior executives and managers behave differently at work and at home. Again, this doesn't mean the Executive Skills are different at each location, just that they are used differently. While at work, the overwhelming majority of executives are good at getting started without undue procrastination (see Survey 3-2 below). However, when it comes to getting started at home for personal matters, it is a different matter, with fewer saying they are good at it. While more than a third say they are *extremely good* at getting started in projects at work, fewer than a fifth are *extremely good* at it at home. And while only one in ten say they are *not* good at getting started at work, three in ten are not good at getting started at home.

There are no substantial differences in the Executive Skill Task Initiation based on the size of the company in which you work. Those in small companies are just as good at getting started in work as those in large companies. And everyone is relatively equally good and bad at home.

In work situations, there tend to be more external influences that create more structure in which people use their Executive Skills. The time required to start work, meeting times, project due dates, and budgets are some examples of the kinds of structure that work imposes. And after arriving home after a very long day at the office you might be a bit drained to start yet something else in the evening.

"Work is so consuming that when I get home the last thing I want to do is projects," says one manager. The reality is that there generally are more severe consequences for letting people down at work than at home.

SURVEY 3-2: Getting Started

At work, how good are you at getting started (able to begin tasks, projects, etc.) without undue procrastination, in an efficient or timely fashion?

Extremely good	38%
Somewhat good	53%
Not very good	8%
Not at all good	1%

At home, how good are you at getting started (able to begin tasks, projects, etc.) without undue procrastination, in an efficient or timely fashion?

Extremely good	19%
Somewhat good	52%
Not very good	26%
Not at all good	3%

VOICES FROM THE FRONT LINES
Getting Started

"I'm very good at getting started. It's the completion where we get bogged down (most times not in our own doings)."

■

"It's not so much getting started, my biological clock seems to work best in the afternoon and evening when I get my most creative and productive work accomplished."

■

"I believe that a leader needs to set the pace, which means being decisive. Getting started for an executive means that his team will progress only when he initiates action."

ONE SKILL SIMILAR AT HOME AND AT WORK: TIME MANAGEMENT

Other Executive Skills are less influenced by external forces, such as the skill of Time Management, which is more consistent whether at work or at home (see Survey 3-3 below). Businesspeople are equally capable in using the skill, no matter the location, with 95 percent of them good at it while at work and 91 percent good at it at home. While at work, there also are more external forces surrounding you that tend to keep you more on schedule than when you are within a "free-time zone" at home.

SURVEY 3-3: Time Management

In general at work (for business matters), how good are you at time management (managing to meet deadlines, keeping on schedule, being on time for things, etc.)? I am:

Extremely good	46%
Somewhat good	49%
Not very good	4%
Not at all good	0%

In general, at home (for personal matters), how good are you at time management (managing to meet deadlines, keeping on schedule, being on time for things, etc.)? I am:

Extremely good	26%
Somewhat good	65%
Not very good	8%
Not at all good	1%

VOICES FROM THE FRONT LINES
Time Management

"Given the new abundance of content delivery vehicles (TV, iPod, web, cell phone, PDA, etc.), it is extremely easy to get off task. Someone always wants something from you at any moment of the day. The great managers are ones who determine what is important, not necessarily what someone else wants from them."

■

"I operate better from an external lens (I am on time, appear well organized) and internally it feels to me as if I am the proverbial duck paddling madly under water to float serenely on the surface. This has been true throughout my career. I guess what that says is that I am organized enough to progress to the top level of the organization and satisfy stakeholders and shareholders. And I still feel that I could do better, be more in control. I think this is the nature of the job and the time constraints we work with today."

■

"Work gets the priority over home matters. It seems work items squeeze into the home space when needed and not the other way around."

■

"Due to multiple priorities and conflicting goals, schedules suffer. Information overload constantly gets in the way of getting things done on a timely basis."

■

"I find that I get a great deal done, across a broad spectrum of things to do, but the tasks seem so insurmountable that things never get done ahead of time and most always just in time. Priorities are sometimes hard to order when everything is either important or essential."

External Influences

There are outside conditions or forces that can cause you to behave more positively even though an activity might tap your weakest skills. These outside forces do not make you better at a skill, but they can, at times, minimize problems that a weak skill might cause. These forces generally are found throughout a business, and can involve people, processes, or just plain hard and fast rules that a company has in place. These forces can be categorized into three elements that come into play at work and that can affect how you use your Executive Skills, even those that are weakest:

1. *Magnitude of Potential Loss.* There could be consequences so great that an action is a top priority, even if you're weak in the particular skill. For example, you could be low in Time Management, but if attending a certain meeting on a regular basis is an absolute requirement for staying employed, you will find yourself always showing up for that meeting on time. This doesn't mean you have become good at Time Management, it only means that something is a top priority due to the significance of the potential consequences. For example, when your spouse tells you that being late one more time picking up your child after school will cause a divorce, you find yourself picking up your child on time. The scope of the potential loss does not decrease the effortfulness of the task, it just brings a particular task into prominence.

2. *Magnitude of Potential Gain.* When the reward is so significant it can keep something at the forefront, even though the particular activity might play to one of your weakest skills. For example, you might have worked an extremely long day and still have a tedious task to do. All things being equal, you would probably either fall asleep or postpone the completion of the task to the next day. However, if someone says they will give you, say, a four-day weekend off if you finish the task today, you buckle down and get it done. The significance of the gain supersedes your lack of stamina and brings the completion of the task to the forefront. Again, if you are low in Defining and Achieving goals you still will be low in that skill, even though you pull through and complete this specific task.

3. *External Cues.* There are external cues that can cause you to deal with a task even though you might be low in the required Executive Skill. For example, if you are low in Task Initiation but your boss always tells you when to get started, you ultimately start tasks. Or if you are low in Working Memory and would tend to forget a particular meeting, you can be triggered by an external cue, such as seeing colleagues heading to that meeting.

By constantly placing yourself in situations that play to your strengths, you'll have a much better chance of continual success. You'll also avoid being regularly assigned effortful tasks, so the work will *feel* easier, since it will be very natural to you. However, there will be times that your weaknesses will come to light and they'll have to be dealt with. In Chapter 4, we describe just how to do that.

4

Dealing with
Your Weaknesses

EVEN THOUGH we have strongly recommended that you play to your strengths in Executive Skills, there are some things that can be done to mitigate your weaknesses. It is only your two or three weakest Executive Skills that you should deal with, since the others are unlikely to hold you back. However, you have only a finite amount of Executive Skills capacity, so there is a cost if you decide to work on your weaker skills rather than focusing on those that are your strengths.

As we pointed out in Chapter 3, using your weakest Executive Skills will be an effortful task for you. Realistically, you have only so much mental energy in the course of a day, and if much of it is used to work on your weakest skills, you may find yourself drained before the day is out. That being said, it's critical that you be aware of your weakest skills and create a plan to deal with them because they'll be the first skills to fail when you're under stress. You probably can think of someone who has gotten rattled and forgotten important things under pressure, an indication that the person is low in Working Memory. Or you may recall how during crunch time before a major presentation, a person weak in Time Management totally lost control of time.

Not Living a Lie

The first step in dealing with your greatest Executive Skills weaknesses is to identify and admit the weaknesses to yourself. There's nothing inherently bad about having two or three weakest Executive Skills. Everyone is essentially in the same situation as you, though each perhaps with a different combination of weakest skills. By answering the self-assessment questions in Chapter 1 you should have identified your greatest weaknesses.

However, there are people who will not come to grips with their weaknesses, essentially creating a house of cards. In interviews, we find a consistent theme of executives and managers saying how difficult it often is for them to convince subordinates of their weaknesses. Granted, in some cases the particular weakness may be misunderstood by one party or the other.

Under pressure, the weaknesses will be highlighted for others to see and can cause major conflict among executives, managers, and employees. The key is for you to identify the weaknesses first (which you've done in Chapter 1) and then follow some concrete but simple steps to deal with them.

The first step is to understand your weaknesses and then identify how they manifest themselves. Being weak in Focus is not, in itself, a problem, but continually getting off track during an important meeting can be. Being weak in Self-Restraint does not have to be a problem, but saying exactly the wrong thing at the wrong time in a big meeting is. You get the idea. And as you might guess, the solutions do not require you to greatly improve a particular Executive Skills weakness, since that is not possible. Rather, they deal with identifying the key issues, problems, or conflicts caused by your weaknesses in specific situations, and then addressing those situations.

Part of not living a lie is to have a clear understanding of how well your Executive Skills match the position you are in. Some of you might already be well matched for the jobs you are in. If you are not, it's worth noting the level of mismatch. For example, if the job requires much time working independently at a home office, you would not be very well equipped if your lowest Executive Skills were Task Initiation and Planning/Prioritization. You would have difficulty as a self-starter and have a tough time figuring how to most effectively spend your day. Results would ultimately catch up with you. The solution for a total mismatch is to work to change some aspect of the job or even the job itself. Otherwise, you'll be living with continual frustration or conflict, or both.

Characteristics of Your Weaknesses

Just as you looked at your combinations of strengths, you can do the same for your weaknesses. For example, if your weakest skills are Time Management and Task Initiation, you would likely be inefficient, have difficulty starting or ending meetings on time, have difficulty meeting deadlines, tend to procrastinate, and be slow to get started on projects. When it comes to dealing with your Executive Skills weaknesses, you should only focus on the two or three that you scored lowest on in Chapter 1, since it is only those that are likely to get you in trouble. Here are typical characteristics of weaknesses associated with each Executive Skill. In a few cases, the same characteristics could be associated with a different skill, which are noted.

- *Self-Restraint*: Has low inhibition, may speak too soon.
  - You can't help re-telling a bad or unfunny joke
  - You phone a client about a proposal after just scanning it
  - You respond quickly to your boss without thinking through your answer

- *Working Memory*: Is absent-minded, needs frequent reminders to complete tasks.
  - You often miss an exit while driving (possibly also low in Focus)
  - You can't remember directions

- When you go shopping, you never make a list and always forget something (possibly also low in Focus)
- You often lose your keys (possibly also low in Organization)
- You say you'll do something later and then forget about it

- *Emotion Control*: Is emotional, sensitive to criticism.
  - You get upset about a memo that implies your department did something wrong
  - The boss makes one negative comment and you feel depressed all day
  - You don't like how your child's teacher handled a discipline problem and you immediately fire off an angry e-mail

- *Focus*: Has difficulty with task completion, is easily distracted.
  - You find yourself daydreaming while checking your child's homework
  - You are sidetracked by office gossip rather than concentrating on the task at hand
  - While working, you're often thinking of something else
  - You run out of steam before finishing a project

- *Task Initiation*: Tends to procrastinate, is slow to get started on projects.
  - You go back to sleep after the alarm goes off
  - You got the memo, but want more details and implications before moving to the next step
  - You procrastinate (possibly low in Defining and Achieving Goals)
  - You need several reminders to cut the grass

- *Planning and Prioritization*: Is not sure where to start, is unsure what's important.
  - You are unable to commit (possibly also low in Task Initiation)
  - You can't seem to make plans
  - You can't decide what kind of restaurant to go to

- *Organization*: Is messy, loses things.
  - Your spouse cannot find a needed file in your home office while you're on the road
  - You routinely misplace or lose items
  - You schedule two meetings for the same time

- *Time Management*: Is inefficient, has difficulty starting on time and meeting deadlines.
    - You are often late
    - In the midst of a very busy day, you have no idea what time of day it is
    - You often rush to finish a report needed for a meeting that is just about to start
    - You're often late picking up your child
    - You have no sense of urgency

- *Defining and Achieving Goals*: Can't focus beyond the short term, loses sight of the objective.
    - Your closest colleague considers you as the start-up person, not the follow-through person
    - You don't finish what you start (possibly also low in Focus)
    - The goals you set for yourself tend to be vague and you abandon them quickly when obstacles arise

- *Flexibility*: Has difficulty dealing with change, has low tolerance for ambiguity.
    - You can't vary from a set schedule
    - When you have a plan in mind and something disrupts it, you find it difficult to regroup
    - You have trouble listening to others' points of view and incorporating their suggestions
    - Once you decide on a plan, you're not comfortable changing it or considering alternatives

- *Observation*: Has difficulty seeing the big picture or recognizing the implications of actions.
    - You don't consider changing tactics after failing at something
    - You have trouble reading a group's reaction to your behavior
    - When problems arise, you frequently decide they can't be solved due to factors beyond your control

- *Stress Tolerance*: Is resistant to change, gets emotionally distressed in a crisis, is uncomfortable with uncertainty.
    - If things happen too fast or too many things happen at once, your anxiety level rises

- You lie awake at night worrying about the next crisis to hit you at work
- You prefer jobs where you know exactly what to expect every day

Don't Count on Negative Feedback

You have to be proactive to identify your weak spots because you can't count on your boss to highlight them, since much of the feedback in an organization is positive. And when it comes to the frequency of that feedback, businesspeople are evenly split, with half getting it frequently and half not (see Survey 4-1, below). But if you work in a large company, you're more likely to receive frequent feedback, and it's most likely to be positive, since more than three quarters of business leaders say their feedback is positive. A third say that the feedback they receive is *extremely* positive. Part of this could be because of fear of offending someone who may be sorely needed to deliver, even if not perfectly. Part of it could also be the hesitancy to deliver bad news, since we know from our past research that delivering bad news is viewed as one of the toughest career decisions managers face.

Receiving feedback infrequently can leave you feeling removed from what is going on company-wide. "I find being in a remote office limits the amount of feedback I receive from my superiors," says one manager who responded to the survey. Of course, not receiving a lot of feedback can be viewed as a positive by many, who feel more empowered when left alone. This does, however, pose the risk to the business that the person may be heading in a direction different from the intent of management. "It is sometimes a disadvantage, and I sometimes feel out of the loop."

The other disadvantage is that your weakness may be allowed to continue unchecked, doing a disservice to both you and your organization. "I believe I (and my organization) would benefit if I received more suggestions for improvement or ideas for development," says another survey respondent.

However, not everyone wants frequent feedback, preferring instead to work independently (most likely those high in the Executive Skills of Task Initiation, Focus, and Time Management). Says one manager who apparently appreciates a high degree of independence: "I am pleased with the level of feedback I receive (extremely infrequent). I like being able to work autonomously and I trust my supervisor to communicate when it is necessary. I'll even do the same for him."

When it comes to negative feedback and identifying weaknesses, there are a few managers and executives who encourage negative feedback. In some cases, providing negative feedback is actively promoted.

"I encourage people to come to tell me what their weaknesses are," says Jill Bemis, accounting director of the Minnesota Department of Agriculture's Finance and Budget Division. "If I see a weakness it might be lack of training, exposure, or experience. A lot of people here have worked their way up the ladder and they've learned to ask for help. The environment here is that no question is a bad question." This openness to dealing with employees weaknesses head-on has helped Bemis keep employee retention high, since both Bemis and the employee are open about what aspects of the employee's performance need to be dealt with.

Of course, Bemis is fortunate in that many of her hires are "accounts payable people," and all have essentially the same job classification and function. This makes it a lot easier to identify what functions a person must perform to successfully do the job. "It's like putting the key into the car ignition," says Bemis. "There's only one key." Bemis' employees must be highly organized and focused to succeed. "I've only had one hire not successful in the last twelve years, and that was my failure because the person was mismatched for the job. I ended up firing him. He couldn't follow order in that he could not recognize order," says Bemis, referring to the employee's lack of being organized, which made it difficult for him to even *recognize* orderly behavior. If a person cannot recognize a desired behavior it can be difficult to achieve it.

By encouraging her employees to identify their weaknesses, Bemis empowers them to be up front with her before she herself ends up noticing the weakness. Once your supervisor approaches you about an Executive Skills problem, it usually indicates that it has become highly noticeable, and is likely now to be a problem—for you. Because we know that managers do not like to deliver negative feedback, once your boss has to approach you it is very likely that the problem has reached a critical stage.

SURVEY 4-1: Feedback

In general, the frequency of feedback I receive from my manager is:

Extremely frequent	7%
Somewhat frequent	41%
Not very frequent	43%
Not at all frequent	7%

In general, the type of feedback I receive from my manager is:

Extremely positive	33%
Somewhat positive	43%
Neutral	15%
Somewhat negative	7%
Extremely negative	1%

In general, the frequency of feedback I receive from my manager is:

	Size of Firm		
	Small	Medium	Large
Extremely frequent	10%	4%	6%
Somewhat frequent	38%	39%	51%
Not very frequent	40%	49%	43%
Not at all frequent	10%	8%	0%

In general, the type of feedback I receive from my manager(s) is:

	Small	Medium	Large
Extremely positive	37%	18%	46%
Somewhat positive	39%	55%	37%
Neutral	13%	18%	17%
Somewhat negative	8%	10%	0%
Extremely negative	1%	0%	0%

As you can see from the survey data, there is more feedback in large companies than in small or medium ones. Although 48 percent of managers in small businesses say the feedback they receive is frequent, 57 percent of those in large companies say it is frequent. Interestingly, while those in larger businesses get more feedback, more of it is positive than in small organizations. In fact, no one in large businesses reports that the feedback they generally receive is negative.

VOICES FROM THE FRONT LINES:
Feedback

"I receive more frequent feedback when things are not going as well as expected. Less frequent when we are scaling new heights."

■

"The higher up you go in a larger organization the less likely you are to receive regular feedback. Experience tells us that manager/ executives need to be self-governing and require less feedback. I disagree; middle managers/executives need feedback like everyone else. Even the CEO needs feedback from the board."

■

"In our organization, we seem to be excellent at praise when things are going well but when things are not necessarily going well we are shy about honest discussion because we fear how tough, although positive, criticism will be taken. We prefer the silent treatment in fear of offending and demotivating the individual. Every time this happens the organization loses."

■

"My managers are not comfortable when it comes to saying unpleasant or negative things and tend to avoid them or generalize. Yet, I need that one-on-one feedback as well, otherwise I am missing out on major personal development opportunities."

The True Failure to Communicate

Now that you've identified your weakest skills, it's worth noting that they can cause issues unrelated to your job or the task at hand. Some of these problems often are misidentified as a failure to communicate or not communicating well. The reality of a particular situation could be that the underlying problem is not communication but several Executive Skills weaknesses that may create communication issues. For example:

• *Flexibility.* If you are low in Flexibility, you tend to be somewhat unyielding in your thinking and approaches to situations. Because you find it difficult to incorporate new information, you can be viewed as not listening well, which is just part of the perceived communications problem. If you are low in Flexibility, you are likely to be uncomfortable with not knowing something. As a result, you might decide for yourself what is best, determine a course of action, and then make it absolute, at least in your mind, without even thinking about it. You would tend to make those decisions unconsciously and rather quickly.

As a result, you might not naturally think of relaying to others that you've made a decision, even though you've already internally committed to it. Then, when others make a suggestion, you quickly dismiss it, since you have settled on a decision already. You then might not communicate any of the details of your thinking process in coming to the decision, since it was made quickly and internally. This leads to a perception that not only do you not listen but do not communicate either, two serious negatives in any business environment. An added consequence is that you can be viewed as not being a team player, since you quickly dismiss or even ignore suggestions from others, since you have already settled internally on a course of action, without input from team members.

Solution: If you are low in Flexibility and are in a team setting, the quick solution is to get yourself into the role of scribe in meetings. Being the first volunteer to take notes at the meeting is the easiest route. This way, you will need to listen to all other ideas and not have time to jam through your own. You should wait until everyone is finished before making any suggestions, which should only be positive, rather than considering your idea first.

• *Emotion Control.* If you're low in Emotion Control, you can become overly emotional. When under pressure, you may get testy quickly and tend to come off as being very short with people when approached. Though it is perceived as a communication issue, it really has to do with you not being able to easily manage your emotions. In most cases there is a specific and identifiable cause or *trigger* that sets off the emotional reaction, which can be seen as negative communications.

Solution: There are three potential solutions to this. One, avoid the trigger whenever possible. If the trigger is another person, then that person will likely notice what looks like your overreaction during a discussion or disagreement with you, though you may not be aware of it. Avoid that person to eliminate the trigger.

Second, identify the trigger and deal with it in advance. Create a prearranged script, such as "I will talk" or "I will listen," and follow it during the actual interaction. You then are prepared to deal with a specific situation in which a trigger is likely to occur. One way to know when to plan for this is to recall instances from your past when something seemed to set you off. When you are entering a similar situation, this would be the time to plan your prearranged script based on the situation. There also are what we call *trigger topics*. They can be subjects in which you have some emotional investment and which immediately stir your emotion as soon as they come up in discussion. The solution is for you to be aware of your response to these triggers and go into such situations consciously planning to monitor your response.

Third, do a relaxation strategy. Deep breathing, counting to 10, creating a mental image of something pleasant, or using a fidget toy are all effective strategies. For example, you could use a rubber stress ball. However, it's important that you directly associate the activity of squeezing the ball with the trigger topic. Using the ball during discussion of the trigger topic not only acts as a reminder to exercise some self-control, but it also focuses energy to the ball away from the potential of an emotionally charged "communication." A good way to identify your triggers is to check when someone feels that you overreacted. If you are low in Emotion Control and are told something that is a major trigger for you, despite appearances, it creates even more of a perceived communication (listening) problem. If you are low in Emotion Control you should avoid confrontational situations.

▪ *Self-Restraint.* If you are low in Self-Restraint, you can be socially inappropriate by acting or speaking before thinking. When under pressure, you may easily say things that are inappropriate, or at best not well thought out or well stated. When the first thing that comes to mind comes out of your mouth, for anyone in the area to hear, it can be perceived as poor communication. It's the typical "ready, fire, aim" scenario.

Solution: The umbrella solution here is to monitor what you say or do and find a way to inhibit it. This is where being high in Observation would be a great help, but if you're low in Self-Restraint you're probably low in Observation as well. The first step is for you to observe the situation to see what it requires. A great solution is for you to write down what you plan to say before speaking it. Another solution is to decide ahead of time what you plan to say and rehearse a short script and stick with it. Writing a script before a sales call is an effective rehearsal and can help you avoid committing more than can be delivered. Just before the situation, where you realize from past experience that you're likely to communicate something you don't want to communicate, remind yourself that you have to control your statements. Creating a visual reminder, such as taking a blank pad of paper to write down what you plan to say can help. The visual reminder can help you stay focused on your Executive Skills weakness as well as provide a constant reminder of how you plan to deal with a specific situation.

- *Focus*. If you are low in Focus you can be easily distracted, no matter what is going on, even if someone is speaking. People low in Focus tend to be poor listeners. As a result, you might tend to ask off-topic questions, or even worse, ask a question that was just answered. Because you have a difficult time staying on topic when speaking, this can be perceived as a lack of communication skill. During a conversation or meeting, you may chime in either at an inappropriate time or with an inappropriate comment, or you may be distracted by some other sight or sound.

Solution: One solution here is for you to take notes, forcing you to listen and track the conversation. At intervals, you should ask a question or make a reflective comment. This is a concept well known in psychology as *active listening*. You can paraphrase the speaker, saying something like "It sounds like the point you are making is . . . ." You should train yourself to take notes and ask questions, which causes less drifting from the topic at hand. Making eye contact at intervals also facilitates listening. However, being low in Focus means you also should try not to stay in the particular situation for an extended period of time. Otherwise, you'll drift off, lending credence to the perception that you're weak in communication skills.

▪ *Working Memory and Organization.* If you are low in Working Memory and Organization you can have difficulty selecting which information to communicate, even though you may be a great communicator. For example, if you are placed in a relatively high-level job that involves keeping your boss informed on a regular basis about day-to-day issues in a large organization, you will find it difficult to succeed in that role. Although your weakness may appear to be a lack of communication skills, in reality you are not delivering the correct information in a timely fashion because you've misplaced it or forgotten something important while under pressure due to weaknesses in Organization and Working Memory. The greatest communication capability cannot mask the shortcomings in those skills.

Solution: The solution for both these weaknesses is essentially a matter of advance planning. The key here is not to try to deal with solutions in real time or spontaneously, because these kinds of problems make spontaneous, effective communication difficult. You need to organize and specify the content, or there will be no logical sequence to the information you want to convey, typically leading to communication that sounds disjointed or irrelevant, at best. Find out what the boss or manager wants or needs to know, and insure the information is timely. You can do this by asking a series of questions: What does he need to know? When does he need it? What is the timeliness of the information? Because the information needed is likely to change over time, the questions should be asked on a recurring basis.

So the next time you perceive that you or someone else is not communicating well, check to see whether it's a case of an Executive Skills weakness. The failure to communicate could be simply an Executive Skills weakness being highlighted. If someone advises you that you need to improve your communications skills, you now know that you need to dig deeper to see what it is that you are not communicating well and map it directly to the appropriate Executive Skills. Then you can check back to the questionnaire in Chapter 1 to see whether the requirements map to your strengths or weaknesses. If the skills required are your weakest, you can select to either modify your behavior or change the environment, both of which approaches are discussed later in this chapter.

Be the First to Highlight Your Weakness

Once you've identified and accepted your Executive Skills weaknesses, the next step is to be the first to acknowledge these weaknesses to your boss or colleagues, presuming they're causing tension or conflict. As you know, some managers are all too good at pointing out your weakest areas, as they talk to you about them and target them for improvement, whether or not you even agree that they are weaknesses. But by the time of that discussion, the perception of the weakness can be quite set in the manager's mind.

Typically, managers aren't aware that these are fixed traits and cannot be dramatically improved, though they continue to try. Once you understand your specific Executive Skills weaknesses, you should beat your boss to the punch in identifying and articulating them. Being first to highlight a weakness provides you the opportunity to frame it in the context of a particular Executive Skills weakness along with its corresponding strengths.

This is a case where you will be buying yourself some time. It's essential that you note something before it becomes an annoyance to others and before it becomes a problem. By doing so, conflict is removed from the situation, as you gain understanding for having a problem and appreciation for bringing it to the attention of your boss. This creates the implication that not only are you interested in dealing with this problem, but also that you're working on it, given your relatively public admission of it. By being first in identifying your weakness, you avoid being called in later to discuss what your boss perceives to be a weakness. For example, if your boss identifies what she perceives to be a lack of communication skills, she could send you for communications skills training—when what you really need is, say, tactics for practicing more self-restraint.

Since you also are aware of your Executive Skills strengths, it's important not to lose sight of those during your discussion of your weakness with your boss. For example, during your discussion about your Time Management weakness, you could also mention your greatest strengths, such as Stress Tolerance or Emotion Control. A conversation might go something like: "While I thrive on and really enjoy the high stress environment here and I am very good at keeping my emotions in check throughout the day, I'm having a challenging time with time management issues, a personal shortcoming of mine."

A Short List for Shortcomings

Since your weakest Executive Skills will always be your weakest skills, you should manage your expectations about how much improvement you can achieve. This is not meant to discourage you but to help be realistic about what you can do with your Executive Skills weaknesses. If one of your weaknesses is Time Management, no number of courses or techniques will make you great at Time Management. However, it may not be that you need to become great at Time Management. You can become more effective by looking at the problems caused by the weakness and addressing those that are most critical. It is an approach to dealing with the effect of the weakness rather than trying to significantly change the Executive Skills weakness itself.

For example, poor Time Management may be causing significant problems at work. You can identify the most critical problem, or the one most significant to your boss. If he tells you that it is essential that you be on time for the weekly Thursday meeting, then do whatever it takes to be on time for that meeting. You can have a colleague call you in advance of the meeting, put a note in a place you will easily and constantly see, or set an alarm. You will be getting to the meeting on time, and perhaps reduce tension in the office in the process. You have not changed your Executive Skill capability in a major way, but you have *fixed* one of the problems it causes.

In addition, when you mention a certain Executive Skill weakness to your boss, that would be a good time to ask him what one thing, specifically, would show that you are "improving" in the area you identified. For example, he might identify that one meeting you really need to be on time for. Consequently, as you arrive for that meeting on time on a regular basis, the net negative effect of your Time Management weakness is minimized. You're not significantly better at Time Management, but it now poses less of a problem at work.

This approach will work with a very small number of issues or tasks. Other than always getting to that meeting on time, you shouldn't expect to regularly remember to file all your reports on time, be on time for every other meeting you attend, be on time for work every day, be on time for lunch meetings, or have the ability to accurately figure precisely how long a certain project will take. However, if your colleagues have become aware of your stated weakness, they can become part of the solution by acting as external cues for you. For example, you could ask a colleague to always make sure she stops in on the way to that other meeting the two of you always attend, so that you go together. This would create a regular reminder for you to attend at the proper time. It's important not to take on the overwhelming and likely failing proposition of being great at Time Management, since it is not going to happen if that is your weakest skill.

As another example, if you're weak in Flexibility and this causes a significant problem in brainstorming sessions, you can work on not passing judgment early but concentrate on how each idea proposed might play out rather than focusing on how obviously great your own idea is. Or if you're weak in Working Memory, when you forget a family commitment, write that family commitment on a piece of paper and place it, with a specific time that you have to act, in a place that is highly visible, such as on your phone or taped to your computer screen. This will not necessarily improve your Working Memory, but you'll be more likely to make your family commitment. You can effectively keep a short list for your shortcomings, so that you can at least eliminate some of the problems a weak Executive Skill might cause.

Change Behaviors: Improving Enough to Get By

The key to adjusting to your weaknesses is to do enough to get by, since you cannot effect wholesale improvement in any of your weakest skills. Otherwise, you'll be spending much time on effortful tasks—your weaknesses—and losing sight of using and leveraging your greatest strengths, the real opportunity. Also, by making a few small but tactical improvements in how your weaknesses are perceived, conflict and tension caused by your weaknesses can be reduced.

You should carefully select which tasks or behaviors you want to work on. Keep in mind that there should be a separate fix for each problem. Making a positive impact on an Executive Skills weakness requires specific, concrete action—what psychologists refer to as interventions. These could include changes in routines, in cues, and most importantly, in the environment in which you work. Using Self-Restraint as an example, you have to create something that gets between what sets you off and your instinctive responses. The old saying of *bite your tongue* would be a very simplistic solution.

Creating a separate fix for each problem means that each problem has to be identified. Each problem is not your Executive Skill weakness, but rather each instance of a problem it creates. Being late for that Thursday meeting would be the problem. Being on time for that one meeting may be all it takes to get by, which would be fine as you mitigate the problem so you can focus on playing to your strengths. If there are many problems that you find need to be fixed, you may have a goodness of fit situation, as discussed in Chapter 3, in which case any fixes you attempt may be either temporary or not feasible.

You should take some time to identify what appear to be critical failures because of any weaknesses you have. It could be that your weaknesses are not causing any problems at all, in which case you are likely to be either in a great goodness of fit situation or in a situation that is rarely under stress, not overly likely in today's business world. Once you have identified the problem:

- *Target the task.* This is something that has to be done, whether small or big. It could be not getting to that Thursday meeting on time, or it could be regularly missing short-term goals, because you're low in Planning and Prioritizing.

- *Break it down.* Take care not to target something that's too big to tackle. If it is arriving late to a meeting because of weak Time Management, work only on getting to that meeting on time, not all meetings. Select the one thing that would make the most noticeable differences to your boss or those around you. You should create a separate fix for each specific problem.

- *Disrupt the process.* Identify your behaviors during the time that the problem occurs. For example, why are you always late for that Thursday meeting? What are you typically doing the previous half hour or hour before the meeting starts? Change whatever it is, and do something else that increases the likelihood that you'll get to the meeting on time. For example, plan to spend 15 minutes before the meeting reviewing materials relating to the meeting. This brings the meeting to the top of your mind, increasing the chances of your arriving on time.

■ *Create new habits*. Changing habits is difficult but can be done. It takes repetition of the new behavior. The key is to put yourself in a situation where you can avoid having to use a weak skill. For example, if you're weak in Flexibility, volunteer to be the one who takes notes at the meeting to help you acknowledge the ideas of others. Better yet, if you're high in Working Memory, offer to write the follow-up report from the meeting, thereby playing to your strength. If you're weak in Self-Restraint, regularly counting to ten before speaking in a group can give you time to think about what you're saying before you say it.

Change the Environment

Although you cannot greatly improve your weakest skills, you can change the environment in which problems occur due to those weaknesses. Identifying your key weaknesses allows you to deal with modifying certain parts of the environment so that your weaknesses can be minimized. You can effectively modify the context in which some problems are caused by your weaknesses so that those issues are minimized.

■ *Create cues*. One way to change an environment is to create cues, which can range from people to things. If you are low in Working Memory, for example, you might ask a colleague who you know is high in Working Memory to remind you a day before a certain report is due.

■ *Use technology*. You can use technology to create cues. For example, computers, PDAs, or cell phones can be used to store information for you. If you're low in Working Memory, writing things down will help you recall what is needed later. You can also use notes placed in a location that is associated with something else but will be highly visible to you at the right moment. For example, a note to yourself reminding you to bring that report back to the office can be left with your car keys the night before. If you're low in Time Management or Task Initiation, alarms can be set to leave for meetings or events on time or to start tasks in a timely manner. You can use databases to store, organize, or sort information if you're low in Organization.

▪ *Make lists.* The overwhelming majority of businesspeople make a daily list of things to do, based on our research, though most do not complete the items on those lists daily. Put on your list the correction for whatever problem on which you are working so it stays on top of your mind.

There are numerous ways you can use your surroundings to help compensate for weak Executive Skills. One person we know who is low in Time Management and Organization relies heavily on calendars, lists, and files to keep track. Her calendar is set so that she is notified 30 minutes and again 15 minutes before a meeting. She also sets up a calendar to track staff key assignments, meetings, and scheduled time. The great irony is that by using those tools, people around her perceive her to be organized, even though that is one of her weaknesses. Following are suggested environmental changes for each of the 12 Executive Skills, so you can select which are relevant to you, based on your weakest skills.

▪ *Self-Restraint.* Think about times that you say things that get you in trouble. They are likely specific situations or conditions, such as certain types of meetings, or even discussions with a certain customer. The key then is to restrict your own involvement in those situations. If it's a specific meeting, see if you can get out of that meeting. If you can't, then sit next to the boss at the meeting, reminding yourself to think before speaking. Create a cue for yourself, such as deciding that before you speak at the meeting you will look at your boss first, thereby causing you to think twice before talking.

▪ *Working Memory.* The best environmental changes here are to use storage or cueing mechanisms, such as PDAs or cell phone alarms. When using a cueing device, such as a Post-it Note, put it in a place where you'll be sure to see it. You also can leave voice messages for yourself as reminders, or even send yourself e-mails, as long as you keep checking for them regularly. The important thing is to remind yourself of things you're likely to forget if not reminded.

▪ *Emotion Control.* One of the most effective ways to manage your emotions is to anticipate the problem situation in advance and plan for it. If you get nervous before presentations, for example, do relaxation exercises before the presentation. Write scripts to say to yourself when you know you face a situation that can bring about an emotional response. It might be as simple as, "I know this can be hard but I can get through it." This is commonly recommended in psychology because it helps create focus on the desired outcome. Also, try to limit the kinds of situations where you expect to have an emotional response.

■ *Focus.* Challenge yourself to complete tasks within specific time-frames, and be sure to give yourself specific start and stop times and track them. Break tasks or projects into smaller pieces and monitor yourself based on each piece, so you have to pay attention for shorter periods of time. Give yourself incentives, such as taking short breaks after each sub-task is completed.

■ *Task Initiation.* Analyze the task you need to do and then break it down so that an easy piece is first. The objective is to make the project or task appear less daunting to start. Set a schedule for starting the task and create a cue to start it. This could be a cell phone alarm or asking a coworker to remind you.

■ *Planning/Prioritization.* Break any project into much smaller pieces based on either complexity or time needed for each. Then create a deadline that seems reasonable for each part, and create a detailed plan for each part. Consider asking someone else to help you create a plan and/or schedule for whatever it is you're facing.

■ *Organization.* Make sure you and your boss have agreed on each of your expectations for whatever it is you're about to undertake. If there are certain organizational requirements, ask for them in writing. At the end of the day, put everything away. This will help begin the next day in a more organized fashion, since you'll have to consciously think of what comes first, second, and next.

■ *Time Management.* As simple as this sounds, increase the number of clocks within sight. This will increase your time awareness, which is a partial step. Then create visible reminders of events and activities you must tend to. You can use the alarms on the clocks or computers as well as asking colleagues to remind you of certain things at certain times.

■ *Defining and Achieving Goals.* Create a way to keep the particular long-term goal front of mind. This could be a one-line description on a board on your wall, a note facing you at the top of your computer screen, or even your computer screensaver. On your daily list of things to do, put your long-term goal as a headline above all the other tasks.

■ *Flexibility.* Try to make as many of your tasks as you can routine. For example, attempt to structure the activities of your day in the same or similar fashion each day, so that you build a steady routine. For example, you might handle phone work at specific times each day, respond to e-mail at several times that are always the same, and even take lunch breaks at around the same time. This will increase comfort for you so that when an unexpected challenge or activity comes along, you will likely have a place to put it.

■ *Observation.* Make a point of evaluating your performance after an event in which you were involved, such as a meeting or presentation. Ask yourself questions, such as: "How did I do?" or "What could I have changed or done differently?" Create a form for you to fill in, or you are likely to forget doing it after the activity.

■ *Stress Tolerance.* The first step is to determine your source of stress. If your stress is related to workload, there are a few options. Trying to get your workload reduced is the obvious one, but this is always at the risk of appearing to be complaining, since so many people at work face daunting workloads. A more reasonable approach is to set priorities, making sure to push less important issues to the bottom of the list. Another solution is to agree with your boss on more realistic timelines for whatever project you're working on.

Complement Your Weakness

The other major environmental change involves partnering with someone who has strengths that complement your weaknesses. Top executives often have personal assistants who are high in Executive Skills of Time Management, Working Memory, and Organization, which can make up for any of those shortcomings in the executive. The assistants can effectively act as an external frontal lobe for the executives, getting them to meetings on time, remembering what briefings to hand them before meetings, and keeping them focused on what is most important at the time. If you are not in a position to have an executive assistant, you still may be able to partner with a colleague or peer.

If you can find someone with a weakness that is one of your strengths, try to agree to help each other in some cases, either by mutual cueing or total supplementing. For *mutual cueing*, if you are high in Focus, and they are not but are high in Time Management, you can help the other person stay on task with regular reminders, while that person can make sure you leave for meetings on time. For *total supplementing*, each of you would use your strength in place of the other person's weakness, a slight variation of what we discussed in Chapter 2 when deciding what role to play when on a team. For example, if you are high in Observation and Flexibility you might assist someone who is not and who is working on a major strategic report or business development plan. The other person might be high in Time Management, Task Initiation, and Focus, so they might assist you in doing a routine weekly report that you always dread. It can be a mutual win for both of you, and the impact of your Executive Skills weaknesses are effectively minimized.

You ARE the Coach

Though executives and managers can also identify your strengths and weaknesses and attempt to get you placed in a great match for your skills, it will be easier for you if you yourself thoroughly understand your strengths and weaknesses and create situations that play to those strengths and minimize your weaknesses. With this knowledge, you can tell in advance whether someone above you is unknowingly attempting to place you in a situation that will require use of your weakest Executive Skills. By minimizing the problems associated with your weaknesses, you can be more focused on negotiating yourself into positions that would use your strengths.

When dealing with your weaknesses, you effectively will be self-coaching. You can set the goals for which problems associated with your weaknesses are the most important to address and how to address them. The objective is to replace an action or behavior that is causing you a problem with one that will not. A key to doing this is to visualize the situation you *want* to occur rather than the one that is occurring. For example, if one of your weaknesses is Self-Restraint and after a meeting you often regret what you blurted out during that meeting, you need to replace that particular behavior. Just picture yourself in that meeting not saying anything until after others have spoken and you have thought out what you would say. Picture yourself waiting. Then create a few words that you can say to yourself, such as "I will wait before speaking at that meeting." Just say this a few times and you actually are likely to find yourself waiting before speaking at that next meeting.

Just remember the steps of self-appraisal, setting yourself a reachable goal, identifying how you will achieve that goal, saying it to yourself, and then doing it. After you have managed this within yourself, it's even easier to identify these issues in others and determine how those others can be best matched to jobs and placed in positions where they can tap into their greatest strengths, which we discuss in Chapter 5.

5

Managing Executive Skills in Others

FACING EXECUTIVE SKILLS WEAKNESSES in others is sometimes more difficult than facing weaknesses in yourself. Whereas the earlier chapters dealt with your opportunities to leverage your own Executive Skills strengths and weaknesses, this chapter and Chapter 6 focus on leveraging the skills in others.

When dealing with your own strengths and weaknesses, you can be realistic about what you might be able to accomplish. You can control the amount of personal effort or sacrifice you're willing to put up with and target how much you expect to improve, even if just enough to get by.

When it comes to others, however, many executives, managers, departments, and even entire organizations tend to want to help someone overcome a weakness, almost no matter what it takes, even though past experience might indicate that it won't work. Part of the reason is personal, since the toughest career decision most executives and managers face involves firing. As a result, they try to fix a weakness in others in order to avoid (or at least postpone) the discomfort of letting someone go. This is less an Executive Skills issue than one of human nature. Executives and managers are simply uncomfortable delivering bad news (except for those who are low in Task Initiation and who therefore are not likely to deal with firing someone until the last possible minute). Additionally, it's much more difficult to recruit new talent than to continue to try to work with the people who are already there. As a result, employees with weaknesses tend to get a second chance, even though that might be putting off the inevitable.

Based on the earlier chapters, you know that it is unrealistic to try to greatly improve a person's weakest Executive Skills. Instead it is much more productive to identify a person's Executive Skills strengths and weaknesses before even considering action.

"We typically trip over ourselves to give people as many chances as possible," says Robert Wyatt, director of information technology for the Society of Petroleum Engineers. "We give people training and coaching. When we find a weak individual or one who is marginal, we give them every opportunity to improve. This is a very people-oriented organization," says Wyatt, who has run the global information technology group for ten years.

Unfortunately, all the training, coaching, and second chances don't succeed because a person's weakest Executive Skills cannot be dramatically improved. So if a person is weak in the skill of Task Initiation and the job mandates being a self-starter across the board, that person likely will fail.

As is the case at many companies, in spite of all the training and coaching that the Society of Petroleum Engineers provides, the individual receiving the additional training and coaching often does not ultimately succeed. "I've been successful zero times," says Wyatt.

Wyatt is not alone. Senior executives and managers tackle the issue of trying to fix the weaknesses in others in numerous ways (see Survey 5-1). The approach used most frequently is to discuss the weakness, followed by providing additional training and then support. As for ultimately getting those weaknesses resolved to the satisfaction of the boss, however, the large majority are not very successful. This is not to say that training in particular tasks, such as tactics to perform a new job or certain business processes, do not work; they obviously can work and often are necessary. However, there is a difference between training aspects of a job function and trying to significantly modify an Executive Skills weakness.

SURVEY 5-1: Weaknesses in Others

In general, when it comes to dealing with weaknesses in others (inability to perform required tasks, poor time management, procrastination, late projects, etc.), what courses of action do you take?

Discuss the weakness	91%
Provide additional training	71%
Provide support	59%
Hold regular meetings	44%
Put on notice	43%
Adjust the workload	40%
Modify the task	36%
Reassign	27%
Fire	24%
Send to workshops	24%
Convince to quit	11%
Issue ultimatum	11%
Demote	6%
Transfer	6%
Ignore the weakness	5%
Force time off	1%
Promote	0%

When you are seeking improvements in weaknesses of others, in general how well do they ultimately meet your requirements/expectations?

Extremely well	12%
Somewhat well	77%
Not very well	10%
Not at all well	1%

Weaknesses in Others

"We try to be clear about expectations and ensure the employees have the tools to do the job. If it becomes apparent their skill level is lacking we'll explore training them or finding ways to bring them up. This may include putting them on probation. After a reasonable period of time (depends on position) if they cannot meet the demands of the position we will let them go. If you don't do this, other employees will quickly come to accept that lack of accountability, perhaps resent you're not dealing with it and make it a broader negative issue."

·

"Managers focus too much time trying to improve an employee's weaknesses rather than focusing in on the person's strengths."

·

"There is a huge difference between lack of knowledge and lack of ability. No amount of training, meetings, and performance improvement plans can help the latter. Sometimes a bad fit is exactly that and the kindest thing to do is to end the pain."

·

"Key is providing relevant direct feedback and then allowing employee to make behavior change within a reasonable period of time. Sometimes additional training is needed, but often it is not. What's needed is a change in behavior, which comes from outlining very clear expectations and consequences."

·

"It is better to address issues head on and try to correct them than it is to bury or ignore them. Sometimes, however, it is not possible to fix. You can reach a person's limits, which means you either lower the mark or, in the extreme, replace the person if the job has changed and now requires more."

·

"Leadership is a people business. If coaching and counseling fail, then a performance plan is designed, agreed to, and implemented.

The results of which signify the employee fit, or an opportunity is created for the employee to seek success external to the organization."

■

"In general, I've found the worst thing you can do is expect someone to improve significant weaknesses. The best for them is to align their strengths with a job that will utilize those strengths. If weaknesses are glaring, they're likely poorly suited to the role, and it's best to help them move along to something more fitting. Everyone will be happier and more satisfied."

Deciding What to Change

Although wholesale change in a person's Executive Skills is not really possible, there are certain modifications that can effectively deal with specific problems associated with the weakness. For example, a person who is weak in the skill of Focus will not ever become great at it, and someone weak in Organization will always be weak in that skill. The question in each case is how significant a problem it is causing and how significant that issue is to you.

Just as there are ways to tweak Executive Skill weaknesses in yourself, there are ways to do the same in others, as long as you understand that there will not be a *major* improvement in the weakness on which you focus.

Trying to change someone else's behavior often appears to be the most logical choice for executives and managers, since the *problem* appears to be all caused by the other person. When attempting to change someone's behavior, all of the responsibility for change lies with the individual. And those changes are in Executive Skills strengths and weaknesses, which are what they are. This is why so many executives and managers find they are not extremely successful at *fixing* a person's weakness, no matter what they do.

However, though significantly more difficult than changing the situation, there are specific steps you can take to change behavior, none of which can be started until you clearly understand the person's Executive Skills weaknesses as well as those skills that are required for the task.

Identifying Strengths and Weaknesses in Others

Getting everyone on the same page regarding a person's strengths is certainly easier than coming to agreement on the person's weaknesses. Take the example of an employee in the State of Delaware Department of Information, who continually arrived late for work. According to Mike Malik, IT manager, State of Delaware:

> "We had an employee who was really, really valuable. We were trying to get him to understand that 'you have to get to work on time,' but he kept being late. We'd tell him that for the amount of work he was doing he could be here eight or nine hours a day. We would say, 'We'd like you to understand that you have to be here on time,' and have him realize the impact if he wasn't. We've been working on it for six or seven months now."

Malik's focus was to try to fix the problem of the employee being late. "We would say, 'we understand' and then ask for a commitment to be on time for certain things," says Malik. "At least now, we get a call or an e-mail when he is going to be late." Malik also tries different tactics with other employees, depending on their strengths or weaknesses. "You can see that even though this is their job, you knew they would be better at something else," says Malik.

He came up with an approach to try to find better fits for people by approaching the people directly. "I'd say, 'OK, let's find out what you're really good at and see how you can do more of that.' As much as I'd like to help people change, you know they're never going to. All you can do is document the behavior and they ultimately become somebody else's problem. You never get them to fix their weaknesses. When you want to get someone to change, you look them straight in their eyes and they say, 'yeah, yeah, yeah,' and they still don't show up for work on time."

Once an Executive Skills weakness is identified and clarified, there are methods to address it. Whether your subordinates use the self-assessment questions in Chapter 1 to determine their own weaknesses, or you or other managers use questions similar to those we list in Questionnaire 5-1 (Executive Skills Profile of Others) below, is really up to you. In either case, the findings should be relatively the same.

Convincing someone that they have a particular weakness can sometimes be challenging. "It's easier to have a third party address the issue," says Donald Ziraldo, president and cofounder of Inniskillin, a high-end winery in Niagara-on-the-Lake, Canada. Ziraldo had one employee who was very good at what she did but could not handle multiple tasks simultaneously. As a result, the serial processor, who needed to process one thing at a time before moving to the next in a series, didn't understand why she would be so overloaded. "Once this was addressed, by using a third-party interviewer, she knew of her problem," says Ziraldo. "The environment sometimes needs to be changed. We assess, and if the person is willing to change, we work with them. The environment is sometimes dependent on other individuals as well within which the individual works. We now give her work when she finishes what she's working on. Higher productivity and a satisfied employee, everyone wins."

A person who may do tasks well but is most comfortable doing them one at a time is likely low in the skill of Flexibility. The person would prefer that tasks be handled serially, and that schedules stay the same once set. In the case of the Inniskillin employee, the person did not understand why she was getting somewhat rattled when handling multiple tasks simultaneously. Changing the situation effectively resolved the issue as well as highlighting the problem for the employee. "If people aren't aware of the weakness or are aware but do not accept it, they could disagree it is a weakness," says Ziraldo.

Like many businesses, Inniskillin has limits on how long an employee can stay without successful corrective action. "We give everyone we hire three to six months probation," says Ziraldo. "However, if after the three- to six-months probation period there are still issues, then by mutual agreement you have to move on."

Determining which Executive Skills are strongest and weakest in others is the same as determining which are strongest and weakest in you, except that it is *you* who answers the questions for the individual. To assure that you are accurate, you also should have the individuals complete their own questionnaires and then compare yours and theirs. The results should be very similar; if there are great discrepancies, you could have a colleague answer the questionnaire about the person. If the answers are significantly different, those differences should be reconciled through discussion before starting on corrective actions. Otherwise, you and the other person will not be working on the issue from the same viewpoint.

QUESTIONNAIRE 5-1: Executive Skills Profile of Others

Read each item below and then rate the item based on the extent to which you agree or disagree with how well it describes the person you are evaluating. Use the following scoring system to choose the appropriate score. Then add the five scores for the total in each category.

Self-Restraint

	Strongly Disagree	Somewhat Disagree	Neither Agree nor Disagree	Somewhat Agree	Strongly Agree
They take their time before making up their mind	1	2	3	4	5
They see themselves as tactful and diplomatic	1	2	3	4	5
They think before they speak	1	2	3	4	5
They make sure they have all the facts before they take action	1	2	3	4	5
They seldom make comments that make people uncomfortable	1	2	3	4	5

Total Score _____

Working Memory

	Strongly Disagree	Somewhat Disagree	Neither Agree nor Disagree	Somewhat Agree	Strongly Agree
They have a good memory for facts, dates, and details	1	2	3	4	5
They are good at remembering the things that they have committed to do	1	2	3	4	5
They remember to complete tasks	1	2	3	4	5
They keep sight of goals that they want to accomplish	1	2	3	4	5
When they are busy, they keep track of both the big picture and the details	1	2	3	4	5

Total Score _____

Emotion Control

	Strongly Disagree	Somewhat Disagree	Neither Agree nor Disagree	Somewhat Agree	Strongly Agree
They keep their emotions in check when on the job	1	2	3	4	5
They usually handle confrontations calmly	1	2	3	4	5
Little things don't affect them emotionally and distract them from the task at hand	1	2	3	4	5
When frustrated or angry, they keep their cool	1	2	3	4	5
They defer their personal feelings until after a task has been completed	1	2	3	4	5

Total Score _____

Focus

	Strongly Disagree	Somewhat Disagree	Neither Agree nor Disagree	Somewhat Agree	Strongly Agree
When they have a job to do or task to finish they easily avoid distractions	1	2	3	4	5
Once they start an assignment, they work diligently until it is completed	1	2	3	4	5
They stay focused on their work	1	2	3	4	5
Even when interrupted, they get back to work to complete the job at hand	1	2	3	4	5
They attend to a task even when they find it somewhat tedious	1	2	3	4	5

Total Score _____

Continued . . .

Task Initiation

	Strongly Disagree	Somewhat Disagree	Neither Agree nor Disagree	Somewhat Agree	Strongly Agree
Once they've been given a job or task, they start it immediately	1	2	3	4	5
Procrastination is usually not a problem for them	1	2	3	4	5
No matter what the task, they get started as soon as possible	1	2	3	4	5
They get right to work even if there's something they'd rather be doing	1	2	3	4	5
They start early as the best way to accomplish a task	1	2	3	4	5

Total Score _____

Planning and Prioritization

	Strongly Disagree	Somewhat Disagree	Neither Agree nor Disagree	Somewhat Agree	Strongly Agree
When they start their day, they have a clear plan in mind for what they hope to accomplish	1	2	3	4	5
When they have a lot to do, they focus on the most important things	1	2	3	4	5
They have formulated plans to achieve their most important long-term goals	1	2	3	4	5
They are good at identifying priorities and sticking to them	1	2	3	4	5
They typically break big tasks down into subtasks and timelines	1	2	3	4	5

Total Score _____

Organization

	Strongly Disagree	Somewhat Disagree	Neither Agree nor Disagree	Somewhat Agree	Strongly Agree
They are well organized	1	2	3	4	5
They are good at maintaining systems for organizing their work	1	2	3	4	5
Their work area is neat and organized	1	2	3	4	5
They keep track of their materials	1	2	3	4	5
They always organize their e-mail, in-box, and to do items	1	2	3	4	5

Total Score _____

Time Management

	Strongly Disagree	Somewhat Disagree	Neither Agree nor Disagree	Somewhat Agree	Strongly Agree
They pace themselves according to the time demands of a task	1	2	3	4	5
At the end of the day, they have usually finished what they set out to do	1	2	3	4	5
They are good at estimating how long it takes to do something	1	2	3	4	5
They are usually on time for appointments and activities	1	2	3	4	5
They routinely set and follow a daily schedule of activities	1	2	3	4	5

Total Score _____

Defining and Achieving Goals

	Strongly Disagree	Somewhat Disagree	Neither Agree nor Disagree	Somewhat Agree	Strongly Agree
When they encounter an obstacle, they still achieve their goal	1	2	3	4	5
They are driven to meet their goals	1	2	3	4	5
They are good at setting and achieving high levels of performance	1	2	3	4	5
They have good ability to set long-term goals	1	2	3	4	5
They easily give up immediate pleasures while working on long-term goals	1	2	3	4	5

Total Score _____

Flexibility

	Strongly Disagree	Somewhat Disagree	Neither Agree nor Disagree	Somewhat Agree	Strongly Agree
They are flexible and adaptive to change	1	2	3	4	5
They generally see different ways to address or attack a problem	1	2	3	4	5
They take unexpected events in stride	1	2	3	4	5
They easily can view situations from the perspective of other people	1	2	3	4	5
They think well on their feet	1	2	3	4	5

Total Score _____

Observation

	Strongly Disagree	Somewhat Disagree	Neither Agree nor Disagree	Somewhat Agree	Strongly Agree
They easily recognize when a task is a good match for their skills and abilities	1	2	3	4	5
They routinely evaluate their performance and devise methods for personal improvement	1	2	3	4	5
They generally step back from a situation in order to make objective decisions	1	2	3	4	5
They enjoy strategic thinking and sound problem solving	1	2	3	4	5
They can review a situation and see where they could have done things differently	1	2	3	4	5

Total Score _____

Stress Tolerance

	Strongly Disagree	Somewhat Disagree	Neither Agree nor Disagree	Somewhat Agree	Strongly Agree
They enjoy working in a highly demanding, fast-paced environment	1	2	3	4	5
Pressure helps them perform at their best	1	2	3	4	5
Jobs that include a fair degree of unpredictability appeal to them	1	2	3	4	5
They are comfortable taking risks when the situation calls for it	1	2	3	4	5
They like jobs where there are not many set schedules	1	2	3	4	5

Total Score _____

Behavioral and Environmental Change

It sometimes can be difficult for someone to agree on any particular shortcoming. "When you find someone with a weakness, it's hard to get them to see that they have a weakness," says Wyatt from the Society of Petroleum Engineers. "I've had limited success with that."

A primary reason that problems arise for an employee is a mismatch or lack of goodness of fit, which we defined in Chapter 3. There can be a bad fit between the Executive Skills a job demands and the Executive Skills strengths the person has. (We discuss leveraging people's strengths by fitting them into the proper jobs in Chapter 6.) Businesses often focus on the weaknesses in others and search for ways to correct them, often with limited success. To eliminate or significantly reduce the problem, an improvement in fit between the job and the person must be achieved. There are two basic strategies to improve goodness of fit by directly focusing on the Executive Skills weakness of the person:

1. *Change the person's behavior.* This would seem logical. The problem usually looks like a deficit on the part of the individual, because the job requires some skill in which the person is weak. If the weakness is significant, then a substantial skill makeover is unlikely to occur. But if limited skill change is sufficient, you can take steps to produce minor change in the individual's actions.

2. *Change the environment.* The second strategy is to change some aspect of the task or situation to better accommodate the individual's skills. We call this changing the environment, and it is generally a more successful approach than trying to change a person's behavior.

Changing the person's behavior requires much more effort on the part of the person. Changing the environment requires much more work on your part, although it produces significantly more positive results.

CHANGE THE BEHAVIOR

When a problem arises with an employee, such as late submissions of reports, the logical approach is to try to change the behavior of the person. The reasoning goes, "If the problem lies with their behavior, then the solution lies with changing their behavior." Although logical, this is not easily accomplished, particularly when the problem involves a weakness in a particular set of Executive Skills. Although mild or relative improvements in a weak executive skill are certainly possible, large, wholesale changes are highly unlikely. So if you can accept only a major change and improvement in the Executive Skill, we recommend options such as changing the environment, changing task demands, or finding a situation that is a better fit for the person. Mild improvements in the Executive Skill might be sufficient to solve or at least diminish the problem so that the employee's value continues to outweigh the cost. If this is the case, then we recommend a plan to change a behavior.

There is a repeatable system that you can use to deal with Executive Skills issues in others. Using Time Management as an example, the following five steps summarize the process:

1. *Select a problem.* Pick one specific problem and describe that problem behavior to the person. Begin work on a specific problem that reflects the Executive Skill weakness. For example, if a person is weak in Time Management and is chronically late for everything, select one specific instance, such as a meeting that she attends on a regular basis but is always late for. Do not attempt to try to get her to be on time for everything, it just won't happen. It's also not really that important for you to get to the reason why she is late all the time. Rather, it is more important and will be more successful for you to focus on the one specific thing for which you want her to be on time for. Meet individually with her, indicate the problem, and determine whether she is aware of the behavior and its impact. If she's not, then explain why it's a problem and what impact it has on the department, organization, or her colleagues.

2. *Generate strategies.* Ask the person to generate some specific strategies and an action plan to address their problem behavior. This should include written steps detailing the specific behavior in which she will engage to resolve the problem. If she can't do this on her own, do it together.

3. *Determine help.* Determine if anything or anyone (e.g., an alarm, a person to provide a cue) is necessary to help the person initiate the new process.

4. *Pick a start date.* Determine a starting date for the plan and decide how the results will be monitored and when the plan will be reviewed to evaluate its success or the need for modifications.

5. *Evaluate.* Establish a specific meeting date to evaluate the initial plan and determine where to go from there. This step should include a discussion of the consequences should the plan or modifications not be effective in changing the behavior. There must be consequences of inaction to further increase the potential for change.

This five-step process has proven effective for behavior change in specific situations or tasks. It is important for you to decide in advance if these limited changes are enough to manage the problem. That is, if the person achieves the results you define, will your needs be satisfied? If they are, then once the behavior change has been produced it will usually be sufficient to periodically check with the employee to monitor the plan, maintain the evaluation system, and periodically provide performance feedback. If significantly greater changes are needed to resolve the problem, you need to consider the other alternative, which is to change the environment.

CHANGE THE ENVIRONMENT

This involves altering conditions or situations that are external to the person to help the person compensate for those Executive Skills weaknesses. There are three general strategies to alter a situation or a task:

1. *Change the physical or social environment.* For example, changing the physical or social environment might be used to assist an employee who has difficulty with the Executive Skill of Focus. That weakness would likely be aggravated by a busy or noisy work area or a near-by group of highly social people. Providing the person with a quiet place to work, especially for tasks that required a high degree of sustained focus, would diminish the problem.

2. *Change the task.* There are a number of ways to change a task to create a better goodness of fit:

- Make the task shorter, either by reducing the amount of work required or breaking it into pieces, with breaks built in along the way. This can help the person with a focus problem, because at the beginning of the task, the end is in sight.

- Make the steps more explicit. The assignment, "Write a management summary of . . ." may work for some, but for those who are, say, weak in Organization, additional structure and guidance are necessary. This might include spelling out the steps to summarize a larger document, or providing an example or template.

- Make the task close-ended. Open-ended tasks can be overwhelming for people with certain Executive Skills weaknesses. They require too much planning, too many choices, or simply too much time to complete. Ways to make tasks close-ended include using checklists or worksheets that help illustrate tasks as they are completed.

- Build in variety or choice with respect to the tasks to be done, or the order in which the tasks are to be done. Have the person suggest ways to alter tasks to make them more interesting or more manageable, or ask the person to suggest the order in which the day's work will be completed.

3. *Change the cues.* Cues or reminders are signals from the environment to do something or remember some action.

- Verbal reminders from a coworker, supervisor, or administrative assistant. An executive or manager might include in an advance meeting agenda a statement such as, "Those attending the meeting should bring with them their report and this agenda."

- Visual clues. These can be any kind of posted reminder. Simple signs or humorous "rules" can be posted where the person can see them. Post-it Notes are the classic example.

- Create a schedule for a specific event or for a block of time, such as across a day or week. The schedule provides an organizational framework and establishes predictability. You can then expect that the person will eventually internalize the schedule.

- Create lists. The list content could be things to remember or steps to be followed. Regularly checking back with him on the status of his list of accomplishments keeps the person focused on what needs to be done.

- E-mail questions. Send regular e-mails checking on the status of the targeted behavior.

These strategies can be used individually or in combination to help improve the match between the individual and the job.

Solutions for Specific Executive Skills Weaknesses

Once an Executive Skills weakness has been identified, a combination of environmental modifications and behavior change strategies will help most people. One way to look at helping someone with weaknesses in Executive Skills is to think of the person being on a journey. The modifications to be made will help them more clearly see their destination, give them a road map, provide helpful signs along the way to let them know they're on the right road, measure their progress, and ultimately shorten their journey. In the beginning, the road map is required so as not to get lost. Over time, they need it less as the route becomes internalized and mental representations of desired destinations with directions become clear.

Although each Executive Skill has unique aspects to it, there are some common solutions that may apply across skills. Following are specific environmental changes and teaching strategies for people weak in a particular Executive Skill. You should concentrate only on those that are relevant for specific individuals, as needed. For example, if an employee is low in Self-Restraint or Working Memory, those should the areas on which you need to focus.

SELF-RESTRAINT

This is the ability to think before you act. It is the ability to resist the urge to say or do something to allow the time to evaluate the situation and how a behavior might impact it.

ENVIRONMENTAL CHANGE

The primary environmental change is to increase external controls to reduce the problems associated with the employee's weak self-restraint. The first step in adapting the environment for such individuals is to identify those situations or conditions in which self-restraint is most problematic. When these are identified, you should:

▪ Restrict access to settings or situations in which the person can get in trouble. A manager who has poor self-restraint may offend coworkers or customers, or make commitments that cannot be kept.

▪ Increase supervision. Adults with impulse control problems may require closer monitoring in certain settings, such as a meeting where the person is likely to say the wrong thing at the wrong time. Monitoring could be something as simple as seating the person next to you in meetings.

▪ Have the person create a role for themselves that is incompatible with the problem behavior, such as being the recorder in a meeting.

▪ Use external cues to help the person control impulses. You and the individual should agree beforehand on a nonverbal signal to alert him to change or inhibit a response. These could be as simple as tapping a pen on the table to gently nudging him at the appropriate time. It is important to agree on the signal in advance so that the signal itself does not cause an unwanted outburst, such as him asking, "Why are you nudging me?"

TEACHING THE SKILL

The focus of instruction should be to help the individual improve the skill relative to a specific situation rather than attempting global improvement. As we have stated, dramatically improving an Executive Skill is unlikely, but correcting a specific problem associated with the skill weakness is possible. For example, if someone is low in Self-Restraint, you are not likely to dramatically change that. However, if there are inappropriate outbursts by her at the weekly staff meeting, that situation can be addressed. You cannot expect to make her better in Self-Restraint, but you can effectively remove some of its effect in this single situation, that of outbursts in that one meeting.

▪ Use a modified role-play and rehearsal. Walk the person through the particular situation, and have her state what she will say or do. Help her create an actual script and review it just before the situation. For example, in the case of the weekly staff meeting outbursts, tell the employee of the impact that her outbursts are having on her coworkers. Suggest that she take a moment before speaking at the meeting and say to herself: "I will count to three each time before I speak at the meeting." Have her practice the script and teach her to repeat it periodically when she feels like speaking during the meeting.

▪ If the problem arises in meetings, have her write down her responses first, instead of speaking right away.

▪ If the problem arises in a sales pitch, advocate using a script. Someone low in Self-Restrain might be inclined to quickly promise too much before thinking to close a deal or make a sale. A pre-created script can prevent this.

▪ If the problem arises in informal conversation, teach the individual to respond with an active listening comment, such as "So, what you're saying is . . .", or ask a follow-up question, or make a statement of agreement. Ask him to recall when he repeatedly said something he later regretted in the course of the normal workday. Suggest that the next time he is in a similar situation that he use the technique of using active listening comments, and get him to practice asking questions before making statements.

Scenario: Brainstorming

Brainstorming meetings are a significant part of Robert's work in the ad agency and are also exceptionally difficult for Robert and the team members. Despite the standard rules for brainstorming—such as getting all the ideas on the table, no judgments, and no problem solving—Robert continually interrupts people and asks them what they meant, or quickly shoots down someone else's idea.

Solution: You give Robert feedback that his behavior is causing others to shut down. Robert agrees that he needs to learn the skill of holding back his responses while still being an active participant and allowing true brainstorming to occur. You suggest a cue for Robert to give himself whenever he is about to speak, telling him to make a loop of private thought that asks, "Is what I am about to say good brainstorming?" If the answer is not an immediate yes, Robert is to say nothing.

The looping helps Robert keep track of the increased ideas that are coming from the group because he is forced to listen more as he continually measures those ideas against what he's thinking of saying. Robert is then able to make his skill-building more public, so that the team allows time at the end of the meeting for Robert to add any additional ideas he wants to contribute. He does this by making known that his Executive Skills weakness is Self-Restraint and he is working on controlling his outbursts to allow others more in-depth brainstorming. This way, Robert can be assured that he is able to get all of his ideas on the table along with the ideas of others, since he has held back during the meeting to let the ideas of others be more fully developed.

WORKING MEMORY

This is the ability to hold information in memory while performing complex tasks, and it involves drawing on past learning or experience to apply to the situation at hand or to project into the future.

ENVIRONMENTAL CHANGE

The way to help people with low working memory is by using storage mechanisms or cueing mechanisms that help people remember information in memory or store it in a readily retrievable location. Environmental change involves cueing a person to retrieve the information on demand or at a set time, typically by using electronic or computer devices. Storage mechanisms include:

■ Agenda books or calendars for appointments and schedules.

■ Notebooks for to-do lists, and electronic devices, such as PDAs, recorders, and even message systems. Some people leave voice-mail messages to remind them of things they need to do when they get to work.

Cueing mechanisms include:

■ Verbal reminders, perhaps from business associates, managers, or coaches.

■ Paging systems.

■ Alarms on watches or cell phones.

■ Visual cues in a prominent place, such as Post-It Notes on a computer screen, or notes on the outside of a folder.

Cueing can include taking advantage of naturally occurring routines in the environment, such as by placing a cue in a prominent place where it's not likely to be missed, like a note on top of the person's car keys. A person who has trouble remembering her calendar can place it on the table nearest the door she always exits by.

For cues to be effective, they should ideally be unusual or unexpected, so they don't blend into the surroundings. Sound cues tend to be more effective than visual cues, because they're more likely to cause an individual to attend to the cue, even if only to ask, "What was that?" You can increase the effectiveness of the cue by having the person practice responding to it.

TEACHING THE SKILL

For working memory, teaching the skill involves instructing the person to efficiently and consistently use the aids and devices that will help them better remember information. Rather than assigning cues, teach the person to design his own cues and to put systems in place to use the cues. The four steps to follow are:

1. Explain the problem caused by the lack of working memory, such as a person always forgetting something at that critical weekly meeting.

2. Provide some options from the cueing list (paging systems, PDA alarms, etc.) or have them generate their own solutions.

3. Mentally rehearse the association between the cue and the working memory aid.

4. Devise a monitoring system, such as later asking if the person used the cue and how well it worked.

> **Scenario: Forgetting Things**
>
> Jason continually forgets things he needs for meetings, such as his action items from the last meeting, the agenda, etc. He even calls his wife at home when he forgets things like his glasses or PDA. People have traditionally agreed to help Jason, but are beginning to see the need to set some limits and deny Jason's requests. Sometimes Jason will miss a deadline or not follow through on a commitment to bring something to a meeting. This makes him feel guilty but he still forgets the items he needed.
>
> *Solution*: You suggest helping Jason put together a list of things he needs to remember to bring to work or to regular meetings. This

begins as a general list—papers, briefcase, appointment book, cell phone, etc.—and you tell Jason to keep this list near the door at home, where he can check it before leaving for work each day. In relaying his daily habits, Jason tells you that he always turns off the coffee pot before leaving home. You teach him to associate this action with the retrieval of his list. You instruct him to put the list next to the coffee pot and learn, through repetition, the phrase: "Coffee off—list on." By being prompted to look at the list next to the coffee pot, Jason can see the items he is supposed to bring but might have otherwise forgotten.

EMOTION CONTROL

This is the ability to manage emotions in order to achieve goals, complete tasks, or control and direct behavior.

ENVIRONMENTAL CHANGE

These environmental changes are designed to help people to more effectively manage their emotions, both positive and negative. They include:

▪ Anticipating problem situations and preparing the person for them. This could be as simple as discussing with the person what types of events or activities cause an unwanted increase in emotions and emotional responses. Identifying likely problem situations in advance can help to prepare for reactions to those situations.

▪ Teaching coping strategies. For example, people who get anxious and overly emotional before presentations or discussions can learn relaxation techniques.

▪ Giving people scripts to follow for specific situations. For example, if a meeting with the person's manager usually causes an overly emotional reaction, tell her to repeat to herself, "I can stay cool during this meeting and I can handle dealing with whatever comes up."

▪ Giving people things they can say to themselves to help them manage emotions, such as the one just mentioned above.

▪ Structuring the environment to avoid problem situations or to intervene early. For example, if people become overly emotional in certain social situations, then limit the number of potential interactions or introduce some structure into the situation. For structure, you might suggest that the person spend a few minutes with each of various groups of people before moving to another group. This way, he'll be focusing more on moving on to different topics in the different groups than on getting emotionally involved in any one topic.

- Breaking the task into smaller steps to make them more manageable. A person low in Emotion Control can feel overwhelmed facing a particularly daunting project. By breaking the project into smaller pieces, he can view each piece one at a time, lessening the overwhelming nature and subsequent emotional reaction.

- Giving the person a break if a task appears to become upsetting.

- Having others model the practice of making positive self-statements. For example, you might have them say to themselves before starting, "I know this will be hard for me, but I'm going to keep trying. If I get stuck after trying hard, I will ask for help."

- Giving pep talks to the person before beginning the task. This and creating self-statements for him can help keep his emotional reactions in check by creating an attitude that the task is doable and realistic. This lessens the chance of emotional build-up during the course of the task.

- Reminding the person that how she thinks about an experience can affect how she feels about that experience. This helps create a positive approach, thereby decreasing the chance of a negative, emotional reaction.

TEACHING THE SKILL

This involves teaching the independent use of strategies like those just described. For example, you can teach someone to identify and use a coping strategy when he encounters a problem situation. You can teach him to break down a task, create a script, or make positive self-statements, as previously detailed. A problem situation is one in which someone becomes overly emotional, even to the point where his emotions get in the way of his effectively performing a job or task. Breaking tasks or jobs into smaller pieces lessens emotional reactions as the specific components become more manageable. A general outline for teaching this kind of skill is:

- Explain the skill to the person, since he may not be aware of it.

- Have the person practice the skill. This could be creating and re-peating to himself statements that limit emotional involvement, such as, "I'm not going to let this get to me."

- Reinforce the practice efforts. Make sure he knows he has to prac-tice creating such scripts and using them in specific situations. The scripts should identify situations that typically cause an emotional reac-tion in him.

- Cue the person to use the skill in real life situations. It's important that he actually use these devices in a practical way in the actual work environment.

- Provide reinforcement for using the skill successfully. Encourage the person by telling him that these techniques will work, and get him to try one to show how effective they can be.

Specific strategies that you can teach a person are to:

- Generate and use self-statements to promote a positive emotional response or an effective coping strategy, such as, "I contribute impor-tant ideas to the team." Just making such a comment to yourself actually helps you realize that you do, in fact, contribute and allows you to feel more positive emotionally.

- Have the person verbalize a goal behavior, such as, "Today I will . . ." before entering the situation where she can display the goal behavior. In a scheduled quarterly review meeting, for example, she might say, "I will not get upset in my review meeting today, no matter what my boss says."

- Use visual imagery. Teach the person to visualize himself managing the problem situation successfully. For example, if he tends to be a poor sport in competitive situations, ask him to picture himself with a calm look or stance. Have him incorporate practicing the skill into something he does routinely every day.

Scenario: Workday Frustrations
Carrie works for a law firm in a small city, where parking is a well-known problem. Every day as she drives to work Carrie thinks

about the company lot and her likelihood of finding a space. When there are no spaces, Carrie must park in the garage several blocks away. And when there are no spaces, Carrie gets angry and often enters the office making sarcastic comments. Though the firm could adopt a better system for use of the spaces, Carrie still needs to learn how to manage her emotions.

Solution: You help Carrie develop a strategy for dealing with the inevitable. Carrie agrees to arrive at work 15 minutes early and park in the lot. If there are no spaces, she will proceed to the garage. Rather than getting angry, she is to say to herself, "If I park in the garage, I get to have some time outdoors and a chance for some exercise, which I need anyway," recalling that she had gotten some fresh air and exercise in doing so a few days ago.

FOCUS

This is the capacity to maintain attention to a situation or task in spite of distractions, fatigue, or boredom.

ENVIRONMENTAL CHANGE

These strategies are designed to accommodate people with difficulty in sustained attention or to make it easier to focus longer on tasks. Solutions include:

▪ Get them to write start and stop times on assigned tasks to help them persist with tasks long enough to complete them.

▪ Use incentive systems. For those who have no interest in their work, extrinsic rewards are sometimes the best hope for success. To be effective, they need to be powerful, frequent, and varied. Examples include awarding small incentives for completed work or for work completed within specific time parameters, or arranging for a preferred or easier activity to immediately follow less attractive tasks. This gives the person something to look forward to.

▪ Break tasks into sub-tasks and give short breaks after each sub-task.

▪ Challenge the person to complete the task within the time allotted.

▪ Use a self-monitoring device, such as a cell phone emitting regular tones, and have the person ask himself, "Was I paying attention?" each time the tone sounds.

• Choose the time of day carefully, such as having people do difficult tasks at the time of day when they are most alert.

• Provide supervision and coaching. People often attend best in situations in which they receive one-to-one attention, frequent feedback, and immediate reinforcement.

• Make tasks interesting, because people work longer and harder on tasks of interest to them than on those they consider tedious, boring, or not important. Ways to do this could include making the task active or interactive, or turning the task into a challenge, a game, or a contest.

• Give the person something to look forward to that can be done as soon as the task is finished.

• Provide attention and praise when the person is on-task.

TEACHING THE SKILL

Teaching people to focus or sustain attention involves teaching them to internalize the externally imposed strategies just described. To do this:

• Help people become aware of their own attention capacity, such as how long they can work before they need a break.

• Teach them how to break tasks into pieces that fit their attention capacity.

• Help them make a work plan. This should include helping them allocate work according to their capacity, and working with them to identify motivational strategies and environmental cues to help them stay on task. Motivational strategies might include finding ways to make the task more active. For example, instead of their just reading a report, give them questions to read for, such as "What in this report can realistically be executed?" Also, encourage them to take notes or use a highlighter when reading, to help them stay focused. Cue them to follow the plan they devised. You can do this by periodically asking how a certain activity in which they are involved follows the plan they previously covered with you.

• Reinforce their behavior by giving encouragement when you see that they are following their plan, which might be tackling the toughest items early in the day.

- Gradually transfer to them the responsibility for making the plan.

- In meetings, have them take notes on information presented.

- Set a goal for the number of times they will make eye contact with the speaker and have them keep track of these. This prevents them from drifting into daydreaming or thinking of issues totally unrelated to what is being discussed. By continually making eye contact, they are forced to stay focused.

Scenario: Missing Reports

Greg works in a call center where he takes customer orders. As his manager, you consistently remind Greg that his daily call reports must be completed by the end of his shift, because the data has to be sent to corporate every night. Greg's excuses typically are that he's overloaded with calls and can't get to the reports by the end of business, or that the structure of the reports is too cumbersome and not user-friendly.

You notice that Greg would finish a call and often leave his workstation for chat breaks. During that time, Greg forwards his call to voicemail or the message center. It is obvious to you that these breaks put Greg even further behind.

Solution: You ask Greg what it would take for him to do the daily reports without being constantly reminded, which has become an annoyance to you, to say the least. After speaking with Greg, you realize that he is not making time for his reports because they bore him. Greg likes interacting with people and gets easily distracted by opportunities to chat and relate with others. You explain that you understand and will work with him on his preferences, but the reports are non-negotiable. You discuss ways for Greg to get them done, including:

- After every fifth call, Greg is to complete some of his reports, making it less cumbersome than doing them all at the end of the day.
- In addition to sending the report, Greg is to bring a hard copy to you before the end of the day, in many cases giving him the opportunity to chat with others along the way. When he hasn't completed the report, Greg, who likes to leave work on time, has to stay a little later to complete the report and leave it on your desk.

TASK INITIATION

This is the ability to begin projects or tasks without undue procrastination.

ENVIRONMENTAL CHANGE

The goal here is to make it easier to begin the task by making it appear less daunting to the person who has trouble getting started. To do this:

- Arrange a set schedule for certain tasks

- Build in a cue to start the task (beepers, alarms on watches, PDAs)

- Break the task into small enough pieces to make the first step look manageable

- Limit the amount of time the employee is going to work on the task and make sure it's a short limit

- Arrange for someone to prompt the employee to start the task

TEACHING THE SKILL

This skill is taught primarily by building a plan around the kinds of environmental modifications just described so that eventually employees can build in the necessary environmental supports on their own. The six steps to teaching this skill are:

1. Select the specific tasks you want the employee to work on, such as one thing that is not being started on time.

2. Together with the employee, make a written plan detailing how she will do each task, so that the individual components make the overall task appear less daunting to start.

3. Set a deadline for completing each piece of the task.

4. Set up a cueing system to prompt her to begin the task. This could be an alarm, an e-mail, or even a phone call from a coworker.

5. Implement the plan and cueing system.

6. Measure the outcome by, for example, tracking the percentage of times she completes the task on time. Also let her know that there will be regular meetings with you to review how often projects are being started on time. This places additional responsibility on her to make sure she pays attention to the cues to start, since there will be no excuses once the cues are in place. It also lets her know that there will be consequences for ignoring the cues and not starting on time.

Scenario: Late Reports

Marie works in a large department in a global corporation. Marie is responsible for weekly reports to corporate as well as for quarterly reports to highlight any budget variances. These reports are very detailed and require input from people in sales, marketing, and distribution. Each week, Marie just can't seem to get around to the reports until the last minute, causing her to work very late one night each week. Because she knows how much time and effort they take, she always finds something else to do, like dropping in on coworkers for a friendly chat rather than requesting the information from the other departments. You recognize that Marie is always saving these reports for the last minute, and that she is obviously tired the next day after doing the reports.

Solution: Together with Marie, you detail all the steps of the report process, including the information needed and where it comes from. You have Marie create a report template that the information can be dropped into. You then have her map a time frame for completing each step in the process with approximate times that she will begin each step. You check in with her at each step, answer questions, and problem solve. After Marie has been doing this over a period of time, you can fade your regular check-ins because a new, recurring habit has been formed. Again, Marie has not dramatically improved her Executive Skill of Task Initiation but she now has a process and steps to start and complete her weekly report.

PLANNING/PRIORITIZATION

This is the capacity to develop a road map to arrive at a destination or goal, knowing the most important signposts along the way.

ENVIRONMENT CHANGE

By modifying the environment, the necessity for people to rely on their own planning skills is reduced. Modifications can include:

- Provide a plan or a schedule for the person to follow.

- Break long-term projects into clearly defined sub-tasks and attach deadlines to each sub-task.

- Create a planning template for each key area. Unlike a specific plan, a template is a model or prescribed pattern that essentially allows some-one to fill in the blanks.

TEACHING THE SKILL

The best way to teach people to plan is to walk them through the plan-ning process multiple times with many kinds of tasks, gradually turning over the process to them by asking questions that prompt them to think about how to make a plan. In the early stages, your questions will need to prompt each step, such as: "What do you have to do first? What do you have to do next?" As the person becomes more experienced with this, the prompts can become more general, such as, "Okay, let's make a list of those tasks in the order in which you need to do them."

Using the analogy of the roadmap can be an effective way to help people think about what planning requires. Using this analogy, have them identify the destination or goal. Then have them visualize the path they must take to reach the destination. With people who are inclined to respond well to visual cues, using an actual drawn map could be helpful. You won't necessarily increase their Executive Skill of Planning/ Prioritization, but you will provide a simple process that allows them to minimize the problems it creates.

> **Scenario: Last-Minute Proposals**
> Stacey works as a financial advisor to a consulting group. She is often called in at the last minute to assist with quotes and the analy-sis of various financial scenarios before the final proposal genera-tion. Stacey is a whiz with numbers but gets very stressed about all the deadlines and pressures she feels are imposed on her by the consultants. She has tried to ask them to involve her earlier, but it doesn't happen consistently. She is at a loss as to what to do in order to get the process of proposal generation under control and more manageable.
>
> *Solution*: You work with Stacey to assemble a plan for the next six months, based on what she knows from the forecasting meet-

ings. In addition, she creates simple planning worksheets for the consultants to use before they engage her in her work, or for Stacey to use as soon as the consultants engage her. These worksheets lay out the steps and the amount of time typically needed to complete each step. This master plan and planning worksheets alleviate a lot of stress and involve the consultants more in the financial aspects of their projects.

ORGANIZATION

This is the ability to arrange or place something according to a system.

ENVIRONMENTAL CHANGE

Too often, the expectations for organization are either ill defined or unspoken. Environmental modifications include better defining organizational systems and making the expectations more overt.

- Make it a job requirement that everything be put away at the end of the day.

- If there are set requirements for organizational systems, communicate in writing precisely what those are.

- Create a designated place for everything and have the person be responsible to always put each item in its appropriate place.

- Minimize the need for organization, such as by giving whatever organizational task must be done to somebody else.

TEACHING THE SKILL

This is one of the most challenging Executive Skills to teach people who are not by nature organized. It requires a great deal of patience and supervision on your part. If you want to take on this task, the steps to follow are:

- Define what the criteria for success are, such as a percentage of material in its place or a rating scale to assess degree of organization.

- Assess current status to create a baseline.

- Meet with the employee to review the organizational requirements that are *not* optional.

▪ For optional matters, discuss different organizational schemes and agree on which one will be used.

▪ Have someone walk through the organizational process with the employee and troubleshoot any problems.

▪ Establish a check-in system and a time frame, including who will check in with the employee and how often. This assures that the organizing process is working and the agreed-to requirements are being met.

▪ Implement check-in and assess its success. Once the check-in system is set up, make sure that it does, in fact, occur regularly and does not fall by the wayside.

▪ Start small.

Scenario: Not Ready for Meetings

Bruce's desk is a mess. There are trays overflowing with papers, various stacked reports, countless loose papers, and pens and other supplies all over the place. The entire office looks disheveled, with files strewn on the floor or stacked atop filing cabinets awaiting a home, and bookshelves fully loaded with books, reports, and trade magazines from past years. The problem is, Bruce is a manager who attends several regular meetings a week, for which he needs to prepare. It seems he always shows up at meetings with either the wrong paperwork, or none at all, because he couldn't find what he needed in time for the meeting.

You don't so much mind how Bruce keeps his office, but his lack of organization creates disruptions whenever he doesn't have the proper materials when called on in meetings. Bruce may even be one of those people you know who always say they know their desk or office is messy but they know where everything is, although you know that they really don't.

Solution: The first step is to determine the meeting agendas and the information needed for a single key meeting. Next, create an organizational scheme and a place for this information to be kept—for example, in a colored folder in a "meeting" tray on the right corner of his desk. Determine how this information comes to Bruce and earmark it for this designated place. At least a few hours before any key meeting, have someone check in with Bruce to see if he has the information or cue him to locate it. Periodically monitor his organization of this information.

TIME MANAGEMENT

This is the capacity to estimate how much time one has, to allocate it effectively, and to stay within time limits and deadlines. It involves a sense that time is important.

ENVIRONMENTAL CHANGE

This involves putting in play systems to make time, including awareness of deadlines and the passage of time, more evident in the person's work environment.

▪ Make time visible, such as placing a clock on a desk where it can be checked regularly.

▪ Make the schedule evident, such as prominently posting it or placing a daily calendar on a desk or computer desktop.

▪ Use a clock with an alarm function to cue for specific events or deadlines.

▪ Have someone else cue the employee.

TEACHING THE SKILL

As with organization, this is a difficult skill to teach, and you should not expect the person to become very good at Time Management overall. If environmental changes are not sufficient to improve the skill to a satisfactory level, then use the following steps for teaching the skill:

▪ Identify the goal, based on the priorities of the organization (e.g., 80 percent on-time completion of tasks or on-time attendance at meetings).

▪ Get a baseline measure (current percentage of on-time performance).

▪ Have the person make a daily plan of tasks to be accomplished, including estimates of how long each task will take and when each will be started.

▪ Have them identify specific roadblocks that interfere with efficient time management (e.g., spending too much time in nonwork conversation).

▪ Discuss and devise solutions to overcome the roadblocks.

▪ Agree on who will conduct check-ins and when the check-ins will be. For example, a manager could be assigned to benchmark whether the employee is, say, getting to a particular meeting on time.

▪ Implement the check-in, and assess its success. For example, you can require the employee to let you know when there are roadblocks that interfere with efficient time management so that later she has no excuse for not dealing with an issue in a timely manner.

> **Scenario: Never on Time**
>
> Josh is always late for meetings. You consider him to be a valued employee and have met with him over a period of three months to tell him he needs to be on time. Josh says he'll try, but continues to be late to meetings and was even late for the last meeting with you to discuss his lateness. Josh typically feels like he's behind and he always tries to accomplish "one more thing" before he leaves for a meeting. Others around Josh are getting more annoyed and they keep complaining to you about it.
>
> *Solution*: Have Josh set aside some work that he will take to the meeting. He can work on that before the meeting starts and not feel he's being unproductive. Have him decide in advance when specifically he will leave for the meeting. This time should be several minutes before the meeting starts. Designate a person to cue him just before the time he has chosen. Have someone record any late arrivals, specify the percentage of times he can be late for meetings in a month and the action that will be taken if he exceeds this. You can designate another manager to do this or even a person who has a complementing strength, so that the two people might even be able to cue each other if they have opposite strengths, as we discuss elsewhere.

DEFINING AND ACHIEVING GOALS

This is the capacity to have a goal, follow through to the completion of the goal, and not be put off or distracted by competing interests.

ENVIRONMENTAL CHANGE

This Executive Skill is often more valued by individuals than by organizations, since there are usually others within the organization who either can, or do, set long-term goals. If this is an important element of a person's job description, then ways to modify the environment to support this skill are:

- If the employee is unable to set and keep long-term goals, you should do that for him.

- Post the long-term goal prominently so that he is reminded of it frequently (e.g., on each page of a daily calendar).

- Hold regular meetings with him to discuss progress toward the long-term goal.

TEACHING THE SKILL

For some individuals weak in this skill, the opportunity to move up in the organization will come only if they are able to become more effective at Defining and Achieving Goals. If you are mentoring such an individual, the way to help her develop this skill is:

- Meet with the employee to discuss long-term goal options and select one to work toward.

- Develop a plan to meet the goal (including tasks and timelines).

- Discuss potential obstacles to meeting the long-term goal and decide on strategies to overcome the obstacles.

- Decide on cueing mechanisms to help her keep the long-term goal in mind and select one or two to use. These could be quick e-mail exchanges, scheduled phone calls, or keeping the objective posted prominently on a white board in her office.

- Set a schedule to assess whether she is following the timeline.

> **Scenario: Novelty of New Things**
> Everyone in the office knows Walter is always the first to get behind a new idea, so they frequently go to him to get his early support for their project of the moment. However, as his manager, you see that

although Walter is so positive on all these projects of others, he isn't meeting his own work objectives. Even worse, you see that at the end of the day Walter has generally not accomplished much. You've mentioned this to Walter in the past and he agreed that he enjoys the novelty of new projects and says he will try to focus more on getting his own work done. However, little changes as the new ideas keep coming his way.

Solution: Meet with Walter and decide on two relatively long-term goals that are key components of his job. Have Walter develop a plan, in writing, to achieve these goals. The plan should specify specific tasks and timelines. Since other employees coming to him with new ideas is a distraction, have Walter decide how he will manage these, such as by making himself available only at specific times. Decide on a check-in schedule to meet with him to review task completion and timelines.

FLEXIBILITY

This is the ability to revise plans in the face of obstacles, setbacks, new information, or mistakes. It relates to adaptability to changing conditions.

ENVIRONMENTAL CHANGE

Often the best way to address the shortcomings of inflexible staff is to work around the inflexibility. Ways to do this include:

- Give the employee tasks that don't require a great deal of flexibility, such as tasks for which routines or procedures can be established.

- To the extent possible, structure his activities of the day according to a schedule or a routine.

- Have him work with another team member who is more flexible when flexibility is required. In these cases, it's important to let the person who is high in Flexibility know that the other person is low in that skill. Otherwise, there can be tension when the flexible person becomes impatient or annoyed with the inflexible one.

TEACHING THE SKILL

Inflexible people often are unaware of their weakness or how it affects their work or their ability to advance. They often also are unaware of how it affects those around them who are high in Flexibility. Ways to help them become more flexible are:

▪ Meet with them to discuss the concept of flexibility. Give them examples of when they've been inflexible and help them identify the kinds of tasks or situations in their job description that require flexibility. Have them identify for themselves when they're becoming inflexible, including what they are feeling, and what their behavior looks like, such as if they feel irritable and they respond that they can't change or accommodate the new demand.

▪ Discuss strategies they can use when they find themselves becoming inflexible, including ways to manage their emotions (usually anxiety or frustration) as well as ways they can step back from the situation either by letting it go or by considering multiple options.

▪ People who are inflexible are good rule-learners or rule-followers. Give them rules for what to do when they find themselves being inflexible. Also give them strategies for coping with situations in which others break the rules. In both cases, these could be things to tell themselves to reframe the situation to reduce anxiety or frustration.

Scenario: Days Not as Planned

Nathan is always a man on a mission. At the start of each workday, he has plans for how the day will go. If he's working on a project, he usually has strong opinions about the course of the project. The problem is, his days and ideas do not always go as planned. Nathan frequently finds himself getting irritated when others request things that get in the way of what he had planned for that day or when people don't embrace his ideas. You have received several complaints from people that Nathan has flared up when they asked him for something needed or proposed alternative ideas.

Solution: Create a rule or job requirement for Nathan that prior to committing to a plan or schedule for his day, he will review the plan with his manager or coworker and earmark any potential conflicts. For these, he will think of at least one solution that accommodates the other person's plan. For team meetings where project plans or ideas will be discussed, give Nathan the job of recording at least three other ideas before giving his own, and establish a general rule that people may compliment an idea or say nothing, but they cannot critique proposals until all are on the table.

OBSERVATION

This is the capacity to stand back and take a birds-eye view of yourself in a situation and to be able to understand and make changes in ways that you solve problems.

ENVIRONMENTAL CHANGE

Modifying the environment for individuals who are weak in Observation involves either cueing them in advance of situations where this skill is needed or debriefing with them after those same situations (or both). This could involve:

- Ask the individual to complete a debriefing form evaluating her performance after situations in which more insight into her behavior would be helpful.

- Meet with her before any situations where past behavior may have caused a problem, and review expectations for future behavior or performance.

- Ask her to approach a problem situation either from the perspective of a coworker or to use a different problem-solving approach than what she used in the past. This will cause her to think of new ways to address problem situations.

TEACHING THE SKILL

The primary way to do this involves giving the employee ample practice in problem solving. Someone low in Observation does not naturally consider many options or even necessarily notice that there is a problem or that something could be done better or differently. Steps to take are:

- Suggest to the employee there are other strategies for solving the problem.

- If he cannot identify another strategy on his own, use a leading question (Socratic method) to help him recognize that there's a process he can follow to solve problems.

- Use this process to generate a template he can use for solving similar problems.

- Give him examples of real world problems and ask him to solve them using the template, beginning with a relatively simple problem that lends itself to the process.

- Prompt him to use this same process as he encounters similar kinds of problems in his day-to-day work.

> **Scenario: Missing the Implications**
> Kurt has no difficulty generating solutions for problem situations or new ideas for product development. He does, however, have a problem evaluating the effectiveness of his ideas. Coworkers have noticed that because of Kurt's difficulty in seeing the implications of his proposals, he is as likely to choose something impractical as he is to choose an effective strategy. Kurt doesn't appear to recognize this characteristic in himself.
>
> *Solution*: Take a solution that Kurt has proposed but which has not yet been implemented. Ask him to play out the potential, long-term benefits and risks of the solution. Then ask him to generate one or two different solutions and do the same thing. If he cannot, select ones that other coworkers have suggested. If Kurt can't see any downside to his solutions, ask leading questions (Socratic method) that will help him see or take one of his previous solutions and discuss how it played out over time.

STRESS TOLERANCE

This is the ability to thrive in stressful situations and to cope with uncertainty, change, and performance demands.

ENVIRONMENTAL CHANGE

This begins with identifying the source or sources of stress and looking for ways to reduce it. Steps to take are:

- Catalog sources of stress on the job and see if there are reasonable steps that can be taken. They can be steps either to reduce the stress involved, such as by building in more reasonable timelines or restructuring the task, or to hand over those aspects of the job to someone else for whom stress tolerance is a strength.

▪ If the stress relates to workload, see whether the load can be reduced by reassigning some responsibilities, hiring help, or dropping unnecessary tasks. Our research shows that the majority of managers and executives spend at least ten hours a day at work, and they have less than an hour of personal time during the course of their workday. The cold reality is that not everything on people's to-do lists always gets done.

▪ If the stress relates to working with difficult coworkers, either confront the issue head-on (by letting the coworkers know what the problem is and enlisting their help to solve it) or reassign tasks or responsibilities to avoid contact with the difficult coworkers. Again, this is an issue of addressing a specific problem that is being caused by a certain trigger or situation and modifying that part of the environment.

▪ If the source of stress comes from being given jobs that are beyond the capability of the person, provide training or reassign the tasks.

TEACHING THE SKILL

▪ Meet with the person and have her assess her stress, and then evaluate if this is consistent with perceptions of others. It's important for her to honestly recognize her stress situation, and using comments by or perceptions of others can help validate it.

▪ Have her rate the level of stress on a 1 to 10 (low to high) scale.

▪ Help her identify typical, specific triggers for stress.

▪ Decide whether the situational triggers can be modified in any way.

▪ Have her select two or three specific stress management strategies (self-talk, visualization, deep breathing) and practice them in low stress situations.

▪ Decide on cues for strategies to be used in high stress situations and rate stress.

▪ Check back with her to see whether she and others perceive her stress reaction decreasing.

Scenario: On Edge

Sally works in a sales department and always seems to be on edge, especially near the end of each month when everyone in the department is under pressure to meet monthly sales targets. As a sales coordinator, Sally deals with many of the salespeople. You've noticed that near the end of every month Sally is almost unapproachable. One salesperson complained to you that Sally yelled at him just for reporting his monthly sales figures an hour late. She told him he had to get his numbers in exactly on time and that she couldn't handle his numbers because they were an hour late, even though that was the first time he was ever late with his numbers. None of the salespeople want to contact Sally personally near the end of the month, so they've started sending in reports and bypassing any direct communication with Sally.

Solution: Meet with Sally and ask her to rate her general level of stress at work as well as her level at the end of the month. Then ask her to identify three specific problems or issues that are most likely to trigger stress or annoyances. Brainstorm with her and decide how any of these triggers can be changed or reduced. Once any changes have been made, have her rate her stress level again and see if it has decreased to a manageable level. Check with key employees to see if they agree. If further work is needed, have her select one or two specific stress management strategies from a list and work out a brief, regular (preferably daily) practice schedule. Use these low stress situations initially and then try them at higher stress times.

Under the Gun

Key weaknesses in Executive Skills come to light in the behaviors of others, especially when things get busy or hectic. For example, someone who is low in the skill of Time Management may have no issues until the end of the quarter when everyone is demanding numbers, reports, and forecasts. Effortful tasks, which we discussed earlier, become very, very difficult when under the gun, because the weakest Executive Skills fail first when under pressure. You probably already know of who around you has the biggest problems in this area. Because sooner or later everyone becomes pressured to some degree at work, you need to get started as soon as possible in identifying the proper corrective action, whether through minor behavioral change or changes in the environment. Of course, the best solution is to strive for goodness of fit, and that can be done when filling a new position or replacing someone, which we describe how to do in Chapter 6.

6

Matching Tasks to People's Executive Skills

ONCE YOU UNDERSTAND a person's strongest and weakest Executive Skills, you can begin to figure out in which situations they would be most likely to succeed. People are likely to do best in a situation where the task requires high use of their strongest Executive Skills, just as they are likely to fail in situations that require high use of their weakest skills. In other words, the person and task are either a good or a bad fit for each other. Knowing this, you can figure out—in advance—whether a certain job or position will be most suited to a particular individual. And when the Executive Skills of a job are a total mismatch with a person in that job, it can be predicted that the person will not succeed long-term in that position. It is almost a guarantee of a failure, though it might never be the person's fault. Rather it's just a bad fit of that person's strengths—or in this case, weaknesses—with the required task or job. These situations can be avoided once you understand how to achieve goodness of fit, as defined in Chapter 3.

Everyone knows instances where someone in a job "just didn't work out." Though a manager may go through the technical steps of removing the person from the job, reasons can sometimes sound somewhat contrived. You might hear a problem described as a failure to communicate well or not being a team player. No matter the given reason, the underlying cause might be traced to Executive Skills weaknesses. In many cases, a boss might deal with the symptoms caused by a weak Executive Skill, never realizing that the underlying cause of the particular action is actually a weak Executive Skill.

A typical track to disaster is when a great salesperson gets promoted to sales management and then fails. The Executive Skills needed for selling versus those needed for managing selling can be very different. Selling typically requires the skills of Flexibility, Defining and Achieving Goals, and Emotion Control. The person with these strengths would be flexible to meet a customer's changing requirements and demands, be able to stay focused on meeting sales targets, and be controlled enough emotionally so as not to overcommit. Managing salespeople, on the other hand, generally would require strengths in Planning and Prioritization, Organization, Time Management, and Observation. The person with these strengths would be very good at setting long-term goals for a sales staff or region, have a good process for keeping track of how everyone in sales is doing, be able to accurately estimate the sales cycle timing to forecast budgets versus actuals, and be able to think strategically with a knack for stepping back to objectively figure ways for the sales staff to improve in the future. When you see a successful transition from sales person to sales manager, most likely that person already had some of these key Executive Skills strengths to succeed as the manager.

To measure which strengths are needed for any job, task, or situation, you can use our Executive Skills benchmark, which appears later in this chapter. You might find that a person's strongest Executive Skills are a perfect match (or not) for those that are needed in a particular job.

For example, a person who is high in Observation, Defining and Achieving Goals, and Prioritization and low in Task Initiation, Organization, and Focus would be a person who is good at getting things done, meeting deadlines, and seeking out opportunities to do big thinking. The person would need structure and support, a routine and a schedule, a paced environment, and a task that matches interests. A good fit for that person could be a high school teacher, whose schedule is fixed and whose time is controlled by external factors (the bell). A match in interests, for example, would be a history teacher with a strong interest in history and in teaching it.

A person who is high in Observation, Emotion Control, and Stress Tolerance while being low in Defining Goals and Task Initiation would be well advised to seek a fast-paced environment, look for short tasks to do quickly, and find an environment that requires a specific and clear task, while avoiding long-term projects. Being low in Defining/Achieving Goals can make it difficult for a person to keep sight of objectives, which are typically required for long-term projects.

Another example is a person who is high in Stress Tolerance, Emotion Control, and Flexibility and low in Time Management and Self-Restraint. This person would need a situation that has variety and does not require a long-term view, such as an emergency room worker. That person would be good thinking on his feet, have immediate goals, and good focus. For the ER worker, critical events would dictate time issues, making Time Management less important.

Depending on the match between personal Executive Skills and those required for the task, individuals will fall into one of three categories: happy, getting by, or failure. Key to managing goodness of fit is that you first focus on matching a person's Executive Skills strengths to the particular job.

How Well Jobs Match

When it comes to matching jobs and people, businesses are good but not great at it. Fewer than a third of executives and managers feel that their department or organization does an extremely good job at matching the requirements of the job with the people in those jobs. The smaller the company, the better the matches. About four-fifths of managers in large companies say the jobs and people do not match up extremely well.

To properly match jobs and people requires a good understanding of the needs of the job as well as the matching strengths of the people, though not all businesses operate that way. "Personally, I prefer to build an organization based on people skills and strengths," says one manager. Any improvement in better matching people with jobs can result in increased productivity because workers will spend less time on effortful tasks and more time utilizing their strengths. It also will take less toll on the individual, because the tasks will be more natural for the person's strengths. From a management perspective, having the right people in the right jobs provides a much better chance of more effective execution. It also means happier, more productive employees, which can result in meeting more objectives and increased employee retention.

Finding the Right Match

When you hire or promote, clearly identify the requirements of the job before looking for people for those jobs. A bad job fit eventually shows up, sometimes sooner, sometimes later. But ultimately every manager will notice when someone is not working out in a particular job. This can lead to one of the most difficult issues a manager or executive faces, which is letting someone go. You can avoid a bad job fit by managing goodness of fit up front, before the person is placed into a job. This pertains primarily to filling jobs that are either new or become open for any reason, such as a person retiring from the company. You also can do it in established jobs, as you evaluate the goodness of fit of current workers and seek opportunities to improve that fit perhaps by moving someone to a different situation or position. This can take considerably more time than perfectly matching a person for a new position, but it can have very positive long-term effects.

General Personnel Management is a decade-old professional employer organization (PEO) with 1,000 employees in San Diego. The company essentially hires employees and manages the staffs for other companies, including the human resource and payroll functions. General Personnel takes extra special care in hiring and correctly matching people to jobs.

"We spend time figuring out their weakness first," says company president Pete Tworoger. "We analyze how they've done in past jobs."

After identifying an employee's weaknesses, which avoids placing individuals in jobs that require those skills, the company turns to their strengths to see where they might be best used. "You can't change weaknesses," says Tworoger. "It's a big mistake to focus on the weakness rather than the strength. You can't find many managers who can walk on water and do everything."

Tworoger and his team have a realistic attitude about the skills of those they hire as well as how to position them for success. "I have some people who are intelligent but can't write well, so I surround them with others who can. We work around people," he says. "Before we promote someone, we look hard to see if the person can do the job, because you can't demote. You have to be honest with them if they are not promotable to the next job." If Tworoger feels that the next promotion is not a suitable position for a person, he tries to make it clear to that person why, as well as why the person will likely be happier not in the new role. He also clearly points out the potential for frustration or failure that the new role might bring with it.

"The hardest situation is the one where a person is trying but not performing. We look to see if there is somewhere else we can put him. If the person cannot be helped, we try to place them somewhere else. As a result, we don't have much turnover. When there is a problem, we look at whether it is the individual or the person he's working for."

It is in both the employer and employee's best interest to find goodness of fit. When assessing goodness of fit, it is important to look not just at one aspect of what a person does rated against his Executive Skills strengths, but rather to look at a broader context of how well the skills match the overall goals of the organization as they relate to the particular job or task.

"We take a look at the person on a holistic basis," says Jeffrey Resnick, executive vice president and global managing director of Opinion Research Corporation, a worldwide research and consulting firm. "People tend to be continually rated against a specific task or job requirement. It is better for the employee and the organization if long-term assessments are made by stepping back to see if the employee's broader skill set and personality fit well with the organization or not. We do a great disservice to employees by not forcing them to make a decision to look elsewhere when that is what is truly in their best interest. It may result in short-term organizational pain, but in the longer term, everyone will win."

In Resnick's experience, goodness of fit issues typically start to emerge in the junior- to mid-level range. Resnick says at this point business leaders have to make some tough decisions. "Historically, we or any organization are not as good at is as we should be. In a humane way, we need to counsel people out of the organization who are not going to make it long-term."

For example, if the company is conducting a tracking study, a system has to be established, which must be well maintained and well oiled. This requires specific Executive Skills strengths, such as Planning/Prioritization, Time Management, Organization, and Working Memory. Excellence in job performance for this type of work does not necessarily imply the ability to move into management, where a broader set of skills are required for success.

Job Skills Profile

Now that you know how to determine someone else's strongest and weakest skills from the Questionnaire in Chapter 5 (Executive Skills Profile of Others), following is a way to use those results against a current job, a future job, a task, or a project. This is essentially creating an Executive Skills resume for a job before attempting to fill the position.

You do this by ranking which Executive Skills are most important for the job or task. First, be precise about what job or task you are measuring. For example, you can benchmark an entire job or just a specific task or project. As in the self-assessment questions in Chapter 1, you must be honest in your answers. If you are an executive or manager defining which skills are needed for a particular job, we recommend that you ask a colleague to also answer Questionnaire 6-1 below for that same job. You then can carefully analyze any discrepancies in your answers to make sure you have accurately defined what is needed for the job.

It is not realistic to expect that a job require that all 12 Executive Skills be strongest, but for any job or task there really will be certain strengths that truly stand out above the rest. Although you may instinctively know which Executive Skills are most required, we have created a questionnaire to help you more easily identify them.

Use Questionnaire 6-1 below to rank the amount or level of Executive Skills that are required for a particular task or job. Although you can rank all the Executive Skills, you really only need to rank the top few, because that will determine which key strengths the job requires.

Questionnaire 6-1: Executive Skills Required for a Job or Task
Place a check mark next to the three executive skills most important to the job or task.

Self-Restraint _____
   This is the ability to think before you act. It is the ability to resist the urge to say or do something to allow time to evaluate the situation and how a behavior might impact it.

Working Memory _____
   This is the ability to hold information in memory while performing complex tasks and involves drawing on past learning or experience to apply to the situation at hand or to project into the future.

Emotion Control _____
   This is the ability to manage emotions in order to achieve goals, complete tasks, or control and direct behavior.

Focus _____
   This is the capacity to maintain attention to a situation or task in spite of distractibility, fatigue, or boredom.

Task Initiation _____
   This is the ability to begin projects or tasks without undue procrastination.

Planning/Prioritization _____
   This is the capacity to develop a road map to arrive at a destination or goal, knowing which are the most important signposts along the way.

Organization _____
   This is the ability to arrange or place something according to a system.

Time Management _____

This is the capacity to estimate how much time one has, to allocate it effectively, and to stay within time limits and deadlines. It involves a sense that time is important.

Defining and Achieving Goals _____

This is the capacity to have a goal, to follow through to the completion of the goal, and not be put off or distracted by competing interests.

Flexibility _____

This is the ability to revise plans in the face of obstacles, setbacks, new information, or mistakes. It relates to adaptability to changing conditions.

Observation _____

This is the capacity to stand back and take a birds-eye view of yourself in a situation and to be able to understand and make changes in the ways you solve problems.

Stress Tolerance _____

This is the ability to thrive in stressful situations and to cope with uncertainty, change, and performance demands.

You can now see the key Executive Skills strengths needed for the task or job.

Task Skills vs. Executive Skills

Now that you've determined which Executive Skills are needed for the job or task you evaluated, you can match a person's Executive Skills strengths against those required to see how well they match. In the left column of the worksheet on the next page, just mark the three skills required for the task or job from Questionnaire 6-1 above. Then, in the right column, mark the three highest scores from Questionnaire 5-1 in Chapter 5 (Executive Skills Profile of Others). This should give you a good idea of how well a person matches up for a particular job or task. You can do this for people already in current positions and for whom you know well enough to accurately identify their Executive Skills strengths and weaknesses.

Executive Skills Required for Task vs. Person's Executive Skills

	Executive Skills Required for Job or Task	Executive Skills Level of Other
Self-Restraint	_____	_____
Working Memory	_____	_____
Emotion Control	_____	_____
Focus	_____	_____
Task Initiation	_____	_____
Planning/Prioritization	_____	_____
Organization	_____	_____
Time Management	_____	_____
Defining and Achieving Goals	_____	_____
Flexibility	_____	_____
Observation	_____	_____
Stress Tolerance	_____	_____

Interview Questions to Find Strongest Executive Skills

Once you know the Executive Skills requirements for a job or task, those necessary skills can be probed through a series of interview questions. Following are interview questions for each of the Executive Skills, with a simple rating guide to give you an idea how a potential candidate might rate on each of the needed skills. Although these questions are primarily for interviews to fill open positions, they also can be used to generate dialogue and feedback with colleagues and subordinates. Typically, once you've identified which skills are critical for the job, the questioning line would include only those relating to those specific Executive Skills. For example, if you've determined that the position you're trying to fill requires the skills of Time Management and Task Initiation, you should use only the interview questions from those two skills.

Depending on the answers you receive, the rating scale can be used to indicate a range from ineffective to highly effective. This system can be used along with your other commonly accepted business hiring practices, which might include references, recommendations, and recruiting. Using this system will provide you with a method to identify precisely which Executive Skills strengths are needed and the ability to probe whether the candidate has those specific strengths.

Based on the interview results, you also should be able to determine goodness of fit in advance, whether low, medium, or high. To make sure a candidate is being totally candid, you can ask for specific details of how a particular Executive Skill was used in a former job or position. If you still are not convinced, you can ask several questions pertaining to a strength, since a person who is strong in a particular Executive Skill will likely be able to give you many examples that will illustrate a pattern of how they have used the skill.

1. SELF-RESTRAINT QUESTIONS

This is the ability to think before you act. It is the ability to resist the urge to say or do something to allow the time to evaluate the situation and how a behavior might impact it.

- Do you consider yourself to be a more reflective or a more impulsive person? Give some examples. (*If the person says they are more reflective, you can ask whether they have ever done anything on impulse and ask for examples.*)

- When an opinion or idea occurs to you in a meeting, do you generally consider its impact on the discussion before you present it? Why or why not?

- Are you considered forceful and outspoken by your colleagues; someone who is likely to voice an opinion even when others might hesitate? What is the upside/downside to this style for you? For your organization?

- What types of situations demand a considered, deliberate, decision-making approach? When do you think speed and action rather than caution are called for?

▪ Describe one situation where your response style did not serve you well.

SELF-RESTRAINT RATING SCALE

Based on the responses to the questions, rate your overall perception of how well the questions were satisfactorily answered, whether low, medium, or high.

Low (Ineffective): Acts before thinking, lacks tact, does not anticipate outcomes.

Medium (Effective): Usually thinks before acting, listens to others, appreciates consequences.

High (Highly Effective): Understands most implications of a decision, is a good listener, makes good decisions based on reflection rather than impulse.

2. WORKING MEMORY QUESTIONS

This is the ability to hold information in memory while performing complex tasks and involves drawing on past learning or experience to apply to the situation at hand or to project into the future.

▪ How good are you at remembering the things you have to do? How often do you forget obligations or things you've said you're going to do? Do you have a sense of the tasks that need to get done before the day is over? (*Although job candidates may be reluctant to admit they forget things, you can probe whether they keep lists of things to do and how much they rely on those lists. You also should ask whether they rely on these lists more when things are hectic, which could be an indicator of being low in Working Memory.*)

▪ What strategies do you use to help you remember (calendars, PDAs, alarms, etc.)?

▪ When was the last time you misplaced your keys or glasses?

▪ Are you able to multitask? Give some examples of how you do this? How good are you at thinking on your feet? Can you take in a lot of information, organize it, and know where you want to go with it?

▪ Do you tend to become totally absorbed in the present, or are you able to keep in the back of your mind other things you need to remember?

WORKING MEMORY RATING SCALE
Based on the responses to the questions, rate your overall perception of how well the questions were satisfactorily answered, whether low, medium, or high.

Low (Ineffective): Is absentminded, has difficulty doing more than one thing at a time.

Medium (Effective): Usually remembers, does not depend on others for cues, is capable of doing more than one thing at a time.

High (Highly Effective): Is highly reliable, always remembers all aspects of the task, may cue others, enjoys doing more than one thing at a time.

3. EMOTION CONTROL QUESTIONS
This is the ability to manage emotions in order to achieve goals, complete tasks, or control and direct behavior.

▪ Are you cool under pressure and resilient in the face of setbacks? Give an example of a time when you bounced back from an unexpected or discouraging event.

▪ Do you consider yourself more task oriented than people focused? Do you look forward to having a problem or goal to work on? How does this affect the people you work with? (*People high in Emotion Control tend to welcome problems and tasks without fear of their emotions getting in the way. They also would be more task-oriented than people-oriented.*)

▪ How do you work with or manage people in your organization who tend to see the glass as half empty rather than half full? (*This can give you an indication of whether the job candidate gets upset or emotionally bothered by others who might be considered negative in the workplace or whether the candidate takes it in stride.*)

▪ When you make a mistake, such as giving a presentation that is not well received, how do you handle the situation? (*A person low in Emotion Control would tend to be upset over such a mistake.*)

▪ How do you think your colleagues or coworkers would describe your style of interaction with them?

EMOTION CONTROL RATING SCALE
Rate your overall perception of how well the questions were answered, whether low, medium, or high.

Low (Ineffective): Is routinely frazzled, is more people-oriented than task-focused, is overly emotional, acts on a whim, is easily discouraged.

Medium (Effective): Can usually resist temptations, is reliable, is not devastated by failure, is optimistic, can handle and use criticism.

High (Highly Effective): Is confident, manages emotions well, is resilient, task-oriented, and focused.

4. FOCUS QUESTIONS
This is the capacity to maintain attention to a situation or task in spite of distractibility, fatigue, or boredom.

▪ Once you start something, at home or work, can you stick with it long enough to get it done?

▪ What kinds of tasks do you find easiest to stick with and which do you find the most difficult to get through?

▪ What steps do you take before beginning a task to ensure that you will be able to complete it in a timely fashion? For example, do you put calls on hold, instruct that you not be interrupted, or move to a quiet setting? (*A person high in Focus can stay on task regardless of busy surroundings.*)

▪ What kinds of things get in the way and make it difficult for you to complete tasks in a timely fashion? For example, being interrupted by others, emergencies that pop up, running out of steam, getting bored, distracted, or encountering an unexpected roadblock?

■ What strategies have you developed for overcoming the obstacles to task completion?

FOCUS RATING SCALE

Rate your overall perception of how well the questions were answered, whether low, medium, or high.

Low (Ineffective): Starts tasks but has trouble finishing them in a timely fashion, does not consider how to structure tasks to avoid interruptions, is easily sidetracked by interruptions.

Medium (Effective): Is usually able to finish tasks in a timely fashion, especially those that are most important; usually structures situations to reduce the likelihood that interruptions will interfere with task completion; when interruptions occur is usually able to get back on track.

High (Highly Effective): Routinely sticks with tasks to complete them in a timely manner, routinely structures situations to reduce the likelihood that interruptions will interfere with task completion, has strategies to combat interruptions and to return to the task at hand.

5. TASK INITIATION QUESTIONS

This is the ability to begin projects or tasks without undue procrastination.

■ Are you good at getting started on tasks right away or do you tend to procrastinate?

■ What kinds of tasks are you most likely to get started on right away and which do you put off for as long as possible?

■ What kinds of things interfere with your ability to get started right away on a task or project?

■ What strategies do you use to get yourself started on tasks, particularly those you prefer to avoid?

■ What happens when you leave things until the last minute? Have you ever gotten in trouble for postponing anything? Has it ever paid off?

• Do you work with people who tend to procrastinate? If so, how do you handle those situations where their work has an impact on you?

TASK INITIATION RATING SCALE
Rate your overall perception of how well the questions were answered, whether low, medium, or high.

Low (Ineffective): Seldom begins tasks promptly, usually leaves tasks until the last minute, lacks strategies for ensuring tasks get started promptly, has no effective strategies for managing her procrastination.

Medium (Effective): Reasonably good about starting tasks promptly; does leave some work until the last minute, but usually for good reasons.

High (Highly Effective): Begins most tasks promptly, seldom leaves tasks until the last minute, has effective strategies for ensuring that tasks get started promptly, has effective strategies for managing situations where others procrastinate.

6. PLANNING/PRIORITIZATION QUESTIONS

This is the capacity to develop a road map to arrive at a destination or goal, knowing which are the most important signposts along the way.

• Please describe what your day at the office looks like tomorrow. What are the tasks that you plan to accomplish? Can you list these tasks in order of priority?

• Let's assume you have several important assignments to complete by the end of the week. When you get to the office, a colleague approaches you to help her with another task that requires your expertise. You cannot help her and also complete your work. What do you feel and what do you do?

• Tell me how you spent your most recent vacation. Did you structure your time or were you just relaxing? (*This answer can give you one indication of whether the person is structured by telling you whether they planned the many details of the vacation or tended to do whatever came up.*)

▪ Talk about how you see time. Do you find yourself thinking about how you will use time, or do you tend to ignore time constraints?

▪ Once you have made a plan and organized your day around getting something accomplished, are you able to change course? Describe how you would reconfigure your priorities.

PLANNING/PRIORITIZATION RATING SCALE
Rate your overall perception of how well the questions were answered, whether low, medium, or high.

Low (Ineffective): Has difficulty determining priorities and making plans, has difficulty meeting both long- and short-term goals, has difficulty anticipating tasks, is easily distracted, can be described as unfocused.

Medium (Effective): Is capable of prioritizing, can meet both long- and short-term goals, can anticipate tasks, is not distracted, is described as focused.

High (Highly Effective): Is adept at planning and setting priorities, can consistently meet both long- and short-term goals, always seems to anticipate tasks, seldom seems to be distracted, is highly focused.

7. ORGANIZATION QUESTIONS
This is the ability to arrange or place something according to a system.

▪ Describe your approach to organization. Do you see yourself as highly organized, somewhat organized, or lacking in organization skills?

▪ Do you feel you have a good system to manage your desktop, your filing system, your computer files, your financial records, or your e-mail or voice mail systems?

▪ What things get in the way of you being as organized as you would like? For example, not *having* the time to get or stay organized, not *taking* the time to get or stay organized, having too much information to manage, lacking sufficient space or the right space to be organized, or working with others who are not organized?

▪ Describe what your desktop looks like.

▪ Have you made efforts in the past to improve your organization skills? If so, what did you do and what was the outcome?

▪ If you were to pick one aspect of an organizing system on which you would like to improve, what would that be?

ORGANIZATION RATING SCALE

Rate your overall perception of how well the questions were answered, whether low, medium, or high.

Low (Ineffective): Has few if any effective organizational systems in place, is unable to maintain organizational systems over time or under pressure, is unable to develop strategies to counteract impediments to organization.

Medium (Effective): Has systems in place to handle the most critical aspects of organization, can recover quickly after organizational systems slip under pressure, can identify impediments to organization and is usually able to counteract them.

High (Highly Effective): Has effective systems in place to manage all aspects of organization, maintains organizational systems over time and in the face of competing demands for time, can identify impediments to organization and has developed strategies to counteract them.

8. TIME MANAGEMENT QUESTIONS

This is the capacity to estimate how much time one has, to allocate it effectively, and to stay within time limits and deadlines. It involves a sense that time is important.

▪ How do you go about planning your day? When do you plan: the day before, at the beginning of the week, first thing in the morning, when you arrive at work?

▪ How do you plan? Do you write it down, lay it out in your head, and do you like to work alone or with others in planning ahead?

▪ What does the plan look like? Is it detailed down to the minute or very specific tasks, or is it more like a broad plan hitting on major goals?

■ Do you focus on specific tasks or how much time you want to spend on different activities? And do you generally link daily plans to long-term goals?

■ How good are you at estimating how long it takes to complete specific tasks or how much time you will devote to tasks? Are you usually on target, or do you overestimate or underestimate how long it takes to finish something?

■ Is there a good match between the tasks you set for yourself to accomplish each day and the time you have to do them? Has this improved over time and if so, how?

■ What do you do when interruptions threaten your ability to follow your plan for the day? What kinds of things get in the way of following your plan and how do you handle each one? These could include previous commitments you forgot about, someone dropping by your office to chat, or your boss imposing her priorities on you.

■ At the end of the day, how often do you feel you have accomplished all or most of what you set out to do? If you are generally successful, how do you account for your success? If not, how do you account for your failure to complete your plan? Do you just push it to the next day, revise your time estimates, or start fresh the next day with an entirely new plan?

TIME MANAGEMENT RATING SCALE

Rate your overall perception of how well the questions were answered, whether low, medium, or high.

Low (Ineffective): Doesn't make schedules or creates schedules that are vague or unrealistic, routinely misjudges how long it takes to complete tasks, schedule is routinely derailed by interruptions, seldom finishes daily schedule, does not adjust well when tasks are not completed as planned.

Medium (Effective): Creates and follows general schedules, though may lack specificity; is usually able to estimate how long it takes to complete tasks; is usually able to stay on track following schedule;

usually accomplishes daily schedule; is usually able to accommodate when schedules cannot be carried out.

High (Highly Effective): Is able to develop schedules that are realistic and doable, is able to routinely estimate how long it takes to complete tasks, handles interruptions so they don't interfere with the schedule unless necessary, routinely accomplishes daily schedule, is able to adjust well when tasks are not completed as planned.

9. DEFINING AND ACHIEVING GOALS QUESTIONS

This is the capacity to have a goal, to follow through to the completion of the goal, and not be put off or distracted by competing interests.

- Do your colleagues see you as being better at starting a task or following it through to completion? What facets of work do you prefer? Which are you better at?

- If you have work to complete, do you tend to get it finished on time or do you find yourself easily distracted?

- Do colleagues see you as someone who can be counted on to get things done? How do you see yourself in this regard?

- It's a beautiful weekend and your family or friends are urging you to join them outside. Your work colleagues are expecting to see the report that you promised would be delivered on Monday. How do you handle situations like this? (*A person high in Defining and Achieving Goals would have figured out how to get the report done by Monday, no matter what. It might have involved working longer hours during the previous week or even over the weekend. The point is, she would have anticipated it in advance, because she would have remained totally focused on delivering the report as promised.*)

- How do you think that your colleagues or coworkers would describe your style of interactions with them?

DEFINING AND ACHIEVING GOALS RATING SCALE

Rate your overall perception of how well the questions were answered, whether low, medium, or high.

Low (Ineffective): Is easily distracted from tasks, seldom completes projects on time, is seen as a start-up rather than a follow-through person.

Medium (Effective): Has the ability to stay with tasks, is able to complete projects on time, can be both a start-up as well as a follow-through person.

High (Highly Effective): Is seldom distracted, even when distracted manages to stay with the task at hand; is very reliable and can be counted on to complete assigned tasks; once having agreed to take something on, stays focused on that task.

10. FLEXIBILITY QUESTIONS

This is the ability to revise plans in the face of obstacles, setbacks, new information, or mistakes. It relates to adaptability to changing conditions.

▪ Would you describe yourself as a flexible person? Do you find yourself digging in your heels when you feel you're right about something? Are you good at following procedures and rules? What do you think of people who are always trying to bend the rules? Give examples to support your answer. What kinds of situations arise in your work that require flexibility? How do you typically handle them?

▪ Do you find it easier to be flexible in some situations more so than in others? Describe both easy and hard situations.

▪ If you find it difficult to be flexible, have you developed strategies that help you respond more flexibly?

▪ If you were to pick one situation that occurs frequently where you'd like to be able to respond more flexibly, what would it be?

FLEXIBILITY RATING SCALE

Rate your overall perception of how well the questions were answered, whether low, medium, or high.

Low (Ineffective): Is inflexible in responding to changes in plans, unexpected events, emergencies, and new information.

Medium (Effective): Is usually able to respond flexibly, especially in situations where flexibility is most important.

High (Highly Effective): Shows flexibility and adaptability in virtually all situations.

11. OBSERVATION QUESTIONS

This is the capacity to stand back and take a birds-eye view of a situation, and to be able to understand and make changes in ways that you solve problems.

- Are you able to characterize the way you think? Describe this mode of thinking. Do you tend to observe the way you think? Are you able to compare this style to other people?

- When you are working with a group of people, do you tend to notice how other members of the group deal with problems or tasks?

- Do you tend to think of yourself as a strategic thinker? What kind of strategies do you tend to employ to help you do this?

- When you make a mistake, such as giving a presentation that is not well received, how do you handle the situation? When you have a problem to deal with, do you try to come up with a single solution, or with several possible solutions? If more than one solution, describe how you select the most applicable one.

- Do you like to analyze problems? If so, do you see any potential downside to this?

OBSERVATION RATING SCALE

Rate your overall perception of how well the questions were answered, whether low, medium, or high.

Low (Ineffective): Tends to make decisions without considering the long-term consequences, uses intuition excessively, tends not to see the larger picture, is not self-reflective, does not tend to generate multiple solutions to problems.

Medium (Effective): Tends to think before acting, usually processes issues rather than relying on intuition, tends to see the larger picture, is inclined to be self-reflective, is able to generate a variety of solutions to a problem.

High (Highly Effective): Routinely processes issues carefully, is analytical and tends to look at all sides of a problem, is able to understand the pros and cons of each possible solution, is clearly self-reflective and has a strong tendency to observe own actions, uses thinking that could be described as strategic, consistently generates multiple solutions to problems.

12. STRESS TOLERANCE QUESTIONS

This is the ability to thrive in stressful situations and to cope with uncertainty, change, and performance demands.

• What kind of work environment do you prefer: one that is fast-paced with a lot of variety but which may also be somewhat stressful, or one where it's easier to stick to a routine and where the stress level is somewhat lower?

• Describe the work environment in terms of stress level in a job that you really liked and in a job that you didn't like. Describe a work situation or a day at business that you considered to be stressful.

• If you have a day where there are a lot of things happening at once and where you're expected to make critical decisions, how easy do you find it to stay calm? If you find yourself getting anxious or stressed, what do you do to help you focus on the job you have to do?

• Do you ever feel like things get too quiet at work? How do you handle it if that happens?

• What kinds of things happen on the job that cause you the most stress? How do you handle those situations?

STRESS TOLERANCE RATING SCALE

Rate your overall perception of how well the questions were answered, whether low, medium, or high.

Low (Ineffective): Is likely to become highly stressed in a crisis situation, only feels comfortable knowing the work schedule for the next few weeks, is likely to become upset after making an error in a presentation or report, may even become upset when asked by a boss to change directions once underway.

Medium (Effective): Tends to be able to change directions when required without becoming unduly stressed, is able to handle a degree of uncertainty and change along the way, remains somewhat steady in a crisis situation.

High (Highly Effective): Routinely handles business without stress; thrives in situations that require dealing with uncertainty, change, and performance demands; remains steady in a crisis situation and is comfortable with changes in schedule or on the fly.

The Case of the Over-Learned Domain

If you come to realize that the wrong person is in the wrong job or that a person already in a job needs help, there are solutions you can deploy, as detailed in Chapter 5. Working with a subordinate over a period of time can provide the results you may have been seeking. If the person has adapted to either the environmental or behavioral changes you instigated, you've saved someone whom you probably considered to be a valuable employee, and the results are finally in line with your expectations. After a period of time, you may begin to view him much more positively. As a reward you may even want to promote him or move him to a different situation. You expect that, now that he has conquered this task, he can certainly take on the next challenge.

However, be careful about moving too quickly. The person may be in what we call an *over-learned domain*. This is when someone, after consistent repetition and coaching, performs precisely what was targeted at the beginning. You have essentially modified the behavior or specific actions of the person and made environmental changes to promote success. Although he is performing what you want, it is because of these interventions. You have not changed his Executive Skills weakness; you have just corrected enough of the problems caused by those weaknesses to create a positive situation. You have created an over-learned domain for the person. This is fine for the specific situation you wanted to resolve, but moving the person to a totally different environment or situation because of the perceived success has some risks. You may find yourself back at the beginning again when you first identified the employee's problem areas.

And Then the Job Changed

Just because a person and a job are a perfect match doesn't mean it will stay that way forever. While someone's Executive Skills remain relatively constant, jobs and tasks often evolve and change over time. Jobs change while the people in those jobs remain the same, at least in terms of Executive Skills. When that happens, it's time to find another perfect fit for the individual, who had been a good fit until the job changed.

It is not uncommon that the role of a person in an organization changes from what the person was hired for. At Bank of America, there are between twenty and thirty call centers around the United States, with certain products tied to certain centers. So when an 800-call comes in, it is automatically routed to the appropriate center. "I was responsible for a portfolio of $50 million in projects, and a person I inherited was great in production and training," says Tom Murach, senior vice president in Customer Service and Support at Bank of America. "We wanted to get the call centers involved. We had to meet certain metrics, but these things were way beyond the capacity of this person. We were trying to have discussions about how to implement different projects, and we needed someone who was flexible and could deal with uncertainty."

"If it is not a fit, you owe it to the person and the organization to find the right fit," says Murach. "This person was good at organization and structure, so we got him a job in Internal Audit. The conversations I had with him were not easy. But the key to being a successful manager is to help people to play to their strengths. Of course, organizational culture has a lot to do with it. The bank here is very open and we have 360-degree feedback."

Robert Wyatt, director of information technology for the Society of Petroleum Engineers, recalls a similar situation in his organization. He had hired a person almost a decade earlier who was well organized and detail oriented, two critical skills needed during that time for Wyatt's organization. "Over a period of time, the requirements of the job changed and the person no longer fit," says Wyatt. "Information Technology operations had grown significantly but the person remained tactical, but I needed him to be strategic."

Sooner or later, an organization will face the situation of dealing with a person who evolved out of the goodness of fit situation, for no reason other than that the job evolved and the requirements changed. This is all the more challenging because it may not be easily understandable when you have to tell the person that he is no longer satisfactorily doing the job that he was commended and rewarded for not that long ago, when, in fact, nothing in him has changed. There are, of course, potential legal implications to some of these types of situations, so it is always important to consult with your HR department in the process.

"The more difficult issue is a veteran employee of twenty to twenty-five years who does not fit because the business has changed significantly," says Jeffrey Resnick of Opinion Research Corp. "An issue is, how will the organization react and the answer is, not very well. If the person does okay, you have to make some accommodation. But you have to be candid with the person."

These are cases of goodness of fit eroding over a period of time. The other key is to align Executive Skills strengths with what is valued most in an organization, which we discuss in Chapter 7.

7

Aligning Your Skills
to What Is Valued

NOW THAT YOU'VE SEEN HOW to determine which Executive Skills are needed for a job or task, and know how to match your Executive Skills against those required for the task, it's worth checking to see how valuable those tasks are to the organization for which you work. We're not talking about *official* company values here, like those stated in the annual report, but rather what an executive, manager, department, section, group, or even entire organization *truly* values in the people who work there. What a company values can generally be matched against Executive Skills strengths and weaknesses. It is not likely that everyone in a department or organization will have the same strengths and weaknesses. This is not bad, because if they did, there would be gaping holes.

Even if your Executive Skills strengths perfectly match the strengths needed for the job you are in, the skills in the job and the skills you have may not be a perfect match to what is truly valued by the organization. This can explain why someone who seems to be doing a good job and is well matched to that job never seems to get promoted or move along the fast track. It could be because the actual activities or tasks being performed, though well done, are not aligned with what is important to the values of the organization.

This can create something like the Peter Principle, in which people hit or exceed their theoretical ceiling. Although your Executive Skills might match the skills required by the job you have, neither may match up with what the company deeply values. So there could be a goodness of fit between you and your job function, but not a goodness of fit between your strengths and what the organization values.

Once you've worked at a company long enough, you generally can tell what the company truly values, which may not always be what it publicly states. For example, a company might pronounce that it firmly believes in work-life balance but then routinely encourage and reward those who work regular 60- to 70-hour weeks. That tells you that the company really values bottom line production or productivity, despite its public pronouncements. You probably know that your company puts a premium on sales if top management proudly states that "We are a sales organization." If you are in a marketing department, you know exactly how your company values marketing, both by budget allocation and perception of marketing department personnel by top management.

What Business Leaders Value

When it comes to what business leaders think their organizations value most highly, topping the list are those issues that deal with customers and the financial bottom line (see Survey 7-1). Companies have not historically looked at Executive Skills because until now most were not even aware that they existed. However, organizations do have general ideas of what they value most, as we have found through our research. The majority of executives and managers rank customer service as what is most highly valued in their department or organization, followed by the bottom line, and then customer relations. Only about a tenth rate marketing as what their organization highly values, and only slightly more rank secure and orderly management. Interestingly, certain Executive Skills strengths can be matched to various business functions and activities that businesses say they value, as you'll see later in this chapter.

Significantly more people in large, as opposed to small, companies rank the bottom line as what is most highly valued. Also interesting is the gap between what the company values and where the managers feel they themselves are providing the highest value. The majority of executives see themselves providing the highest value with customer service, followed by customer relations, and then creativity and new ideas. There is an obvious gap between the bottom line being one of the most valued by the majority of businesses and it not being one of the top areas where the businesspeople feel they provide the highest value. Whereas 63 percent say their department or organization most values the bottom line, only 39 percent say that is the area where they provide the most value. The simple point here is that there are differences between what companies value most and where individuals in those organizations feel they provide the highest value.

In a separate survey, executives and managers say their organization would value them more if they, in order, increased revenue, did more with less, communicated more, and cut costs. This shows that, at the least, business leaders have a perspective on what their organization values, which ultimately can be linked to Executive Skills strengths, as you will see.

SURVEY 7-1: Values
What does your department and/or organization value most highly?

Customer service	65%
Bottom line	63%
Customer relations	57%
Service	38%
Communications	35%
Creativity, new ideas	34%
Production, delivery	32%
Sales	30%

Secure and orderly management	12%
Marketing	11%

In which areas do you feel you provide the highest value?

Customer service	58%
Customer relations	50%
Creativity, new ideas	50%
Communications	40%
Bottom line	39%
Service	34%
Production, delivery	27%
Sales	21%
Secure and orderly management	20%
Marketing	16%

By size of company, what does your department and/or organization value most highly?

	Small	Medium	Large
Customer relations	68%	48%	44%
Customer service	67%	67%	56%
Bottom line	47%	77%	84%
Creativity, new ideas	41%	29%	22%
Service	38%	33%	44%
Communications	34%	44%	25%
Production, delivery	33%	40%	20%
Sales	30%	27%	31%
Secure and orderly management	11%	15%	13%
Marketing	8%	13%	13%

By size of company, in which areas do you feel you provide the highest value?

	Small	Medium	Large
Customer service	58%	58%	59%
Customer relations	57%	48%	41%
Creativity, new ideas	49%	48%	56%
Bottom line	35%	38%	53%
Communications	35%	54%	34%
Service	33%	35%	38%
Production, delivery	28%	23%	34%
Marketing	22%	8%	13%
Sales	23%	23%	13%
Secure and orderly management	17%	27%	19%

VOICE FROM THE FRONT LINES
What Is Highly Valued

"If the product or service is delivered with less than stellar customer service or without good customer relations, what good is it?"

■

"Above those, my organization values taking advantage of opportunities. Growth is difficult because overall market size is mature. When an acquisition opportunity becomes real, it takes precedence on everything else."

■

"Our philosophy is the client is king. It drives all of our decisions."

■

"If we do well on the service side, we tend to hit bottom line. Our board highly values quality of delivery, but doesn't get to that topic until assessing whether we are hitting our numbers. We live in a bottom line world."

Task Skills Most Valued Compared to Your Executive Skills

So how do you know which Executive Skills your department or organization truly values? If you've worked in your business for some length of time, you probably already know, though you may have never really thought about it. When conversing with colleagues, you may come to the same conclusions. For example, based on past actions you know that your organization appreciates, say, Flexibility and Stress Tolerance. If the leadership strongly encourages taking risks and making frequent changes in course, it is likely they value these skills.

In the worksheet below, assess how your skills and those required for the job compare to what is most valued by your business. In the first column, simply place a check mark at your three highest Executive Skills (from the self-assessment questions in Chapter 1). In the second column, mark the highest skills required for your job or task from Questionnaire 6-1 in Chapter 6 (Executive Skills Required for Job or Task). In the third column, place a check mark next to what your organization values. You now can assess the alignment between your Executive Skills, those skills required for the job you are in, and those skills valued by the organization for which you work.

Executive Skills vs. Skills Most Valued by Company

	Your Executive Skills Level	Executive Skills Required for Job or Task	Executive Skills Truly Valued by Company
Self-Restraint	_____	_____	_____
Working Memory	_____	_____	_____
Emotion Control	_____	_____	_____
Focus	_____	_____	_____
Task Initiation	_____	_____	_____
Planning/Prioritization	_____	_____	_____
Organization	_____	_____	_____
Time Management	_____	_____	_____
Defining/Achieving Goals	_____	_____	_____
Flexibility	_____	_____	_____

Observation　　　　　_____　　　_____　　　_____

Stress Tolerance　　　_____　　　_____　　　_____

Long-Term Goodness of Fit

Besides knowing how well your Executive Skills line up to your job, knowing how well they align with what your company values might give you a longer-term view of your prospects for success within the organization. Although your current job might not be a perfect match for your strongest skills, that can change as you move through your career, especially if you play to your strengths, as we discussed in Chapter 3. You may find that a promotion or department transfer moves you into a better goodness-of-fit situation, at least as it relates to the job or task. However, your company values are likely to be steadier than a particular job, and if your strengths are aligned with those, you have a good chance for goodness of fit elsewhere in the organization, not just in your current position.

You also can determine how your colleagues align, since you can assess their strengths and weaknesses using Questionnaire 5-1 in Chapter 5 (Executive Skills Profile of Others), and then pair those results with those from this chapter relating to what the business most highly values.

Matching Values to Your Skills

It isn't likely that an organization would state that it highly values specific Executive Skills. It is more likely that it would state that it values certain functions or goals, such as customer service or the bottom line. However, there are combinations of Executive Skills that underlie these functions, and once you know them you can see where you might fit against those values. There's a method you can use to quickly check whether your greatest strengths in Executive Skills are aligned with what matters to your organization. Following are some general guidelines that highlight what an organization might value, along with the Executive Skills strengths that would most match that value. Earlier in the book, we identified which combinations of Executive Skills strengths would likely be needed for certain types of situations, such as strategy or detail work. Here is another way to look at which Executive Skills strengths would be most suitable for specific job functions valued by an organization:

- *Creativity, New Ideas.* These could be jobs that involve product development, coming up with new ideas, such as research and development or new business development, where new business opportunities are explored. *High skills:* Flexibility and Observation.

- *Production, Delivery.* This is where the organization places a high value on execution, or getting things done and out the door on time. *High skills:* Task Initiation, Defining and Achieving Goals, and Time Management.

- *Customer Relations.* This could be the value a company places in its top salespeople, who manage corporate accounts. It also could involve anyone who deals directly with the customer or client, often when the customer has a complaint. *High skills:* Flexibility, Emotion Control.

- *Bottom Line.* There are some departments and organizations that are essentially numbers driven, placing a premium on making the numbers above all else. You will know it if you work in one of these departments or businesses. *High skills:* Defining and Achieving Goals, Focus, Planning and Prioritization.

- *Secure and Orderly Management.* This is where the organization highly values certain routines, such as always opening a bank on time and operating it in a predictable and familiar-to-customers manner. *High skills:* Organization, Time Management.

- *Marketing.* Businesses that place a premium on marketing tend to have marketing departments whose less rigid environments make them receptive to new ideas. *High skills:* Flexibility, Planning/Prioritization, Observation.

- *Sales.* If you're in sales you likely already know how what you do is valued within the organization. No matter the size of business, its sales department is one of the easier areas for determining its value to the organization. You know, for example, that when the chief executive personally calls a salesperson or sales manager after a significant sale that sales is highly appreciated and valued. *High skills:* Flexibility, Emotion Control, Defining and Achieving Goals.

▪ *Customer Service.* These could be the jobs that range from fielding customer calls, such as in call centers, or even customer service agents, or the last-line-of-defense people before losing a customer. They also could be proactive customer service representatives who can deal with all types of customers. *High skills*: Self-Restraint, Flexibility, Emotion Control, Task Initiation.

▪ *Service.* These could be positions that involve taking care of servicing something after an initial sale. Unlike customer service, where customers may be contacting someone to answer a complaint, service could be inherent in an entire organization, such as wireless phone carriers, which exist to provide continuing service to customers. Dealing in service is sort of like selling something that cannot be seen, and you should know if your company puts a premium on service. One way to know if service is highly valued would be if top management constantly preaches internally, "We are all about service." *High skills*: Task Initiation, Defining and Achieving Goals.

▪ *Communications.* The ability to communicate well may not be tied to any specific job, title, or function, but could be highly valued in an organization where informing and the sharing of ideas are paramount. *High skills*: Planning/Prioritization, Defining and Achieving Goals, Organization.

▪ *Project Management.* These functions in an organization could be official project managers, which would involve successfully managing a project within the confines of time, cost, and scope, integrated with quality. These would be temporary activities, with a beginning and well-defined end, with the goal of creating a product or service. *High Skills*: Planning and Prioritization, Defining and Achieving Goals, Emotion Control.

The Halo Effect: Look More Valuable

If for whatever reasons your strengths are not a match for the values of the organization, all is not lost. You can find something in your strengths that is valued and make yourself stand out in those areas. For example, you can identify two things that your company values most, and then determine how within those things you could make an impact using your strongest Executive Skills. If your company most values marketing, for example, and you are not strong in the skills associated with that (i.e., Flexibility, Planning and Prioritization, and Observation), you can use other strengths you have. You might be high in Time Management, so you could use that to assist or contribute to someone who is high in the other set of skills. You could use your skill strength to assure that the schedule for an important marketing deadline is met, since a person with the other strengths is not likely to also be high in Time Management.

After your assistance assures that the marketing deadline is met, you should let it be known how you helped contribute to the marketing effort. Since the particular company highly values marketing, you receive the halo effect of the marketing effort win by the other person. You become associated with contributing to what the business most values even though you possess none of the Executive Skills strengths that match those values.

In another example, the organization may highly value project management, but you are low in the Executive Skills associated with that (Planning and Prioritization, Defining and Achieving Goals, Emotion Control). Presuming you are high in Flexibility and Observation, you could contribute creative ideas to the project management team that it might not likely consider because of its focus on execution. You might suggest a new approach to an internal project that team leaders had not thought of. Once the approach is adopted, make sure the project team leader understands that your idea helped to streamline the project, contributing to the on-time delivery of the project. You then receive the halo effect for on-time performance of the project management team, even though you are low in Time Management.

For whatever teams you're on, whether it be a management team, project team, or process team, it is important to identify who on the team is most closely aligned with the company's greatest values and then use your greatest strengths to contribute to that person's major activities within the group. This will assure that you become associated with delivering consistently with the company values on a regular basis, which should become obvious to others. But even if it goes unnoticed, your efforts will generally go toward improving the business by increasing efficiency or quality, even if in only one area.

Of course, there's a difference between boasting and taking credit for your contributions. You or someone you know probably has at one time or another been overlooked when a team leader failed to acknowledge a contribution. It could have been an oversight, a lack of time, or simply someone else trying to take credit all alone.

Another reason for not receiving credit from a team leader could be that she has a very different Executive Skill set and is most conscious of only those skills. For example, if she is strong in Task Initiation, Time Management, and Focus, she might commend others after the meeting for doing such a great job of staying on task and getting a proposal finished on time. She is focused on the values of her particular set of skills. Meanwhile, if your strengths are Observation and Flexibility, you likely made significant contributions to the ideas themselves, but they went unnoticed. Maybe the team leader does not consider idea creation as a critical component of what the team accomplished; it just is not high on her radar.

When your contributions are blatantly ignored, you can highlight them without looking like a braggart. Approach the team leader and explain, on her terms, how you contributed. However, rather than highlighting how great your ideas were, instead make the connection to how your coming up with the idea allowed the proposal to be completed on time. The team leader, being so appreciative of time issues, can then view your contribution within her world. The other approach, of course, is to educate the team leader about how different Executive Skills go into the tasks. You can even use the scenario we just described as an example. And the next time there's another such meeting, start differently by identifying up front that there are certain skills that will be required for the group to come up with a solution. And be sure that you know in advance how your strongest Executive Skills fit in the mix.

Executive Skills Alignment as a Career Strategy

Aligning your strengths to jobs and company values can present a winning strategy for your entire career. If you think back about jobs and positions you've held, you might recall one that felt extremely difficult for you, or tougher than you thought it should have been. It could have been one that not only did *not* play to your strengths, but also required Executive Skills that were among your weakest. You also might recall an opposite situation, where the work was pleasant and felt easier to execute. That might have been a position that played to your strengths, a goodness of fit situation.

If you've been in one position for a very long time, there always will be the chance that the leadership of your organization will one day take dramatic steps in an attempt to better match people and jobs. Sometimes this is because of a merger, new management, increasing customer demands, requirements to improve the bottom line, or any number of other reasons, some of which may never even be stated.

At Marlboro Manufacturing in Alliance, Ohio, Sly Kodrin was hired as vice president of operations, reporting directly to the president of the family-owned business. Kodrin was brought in as a change agent for the multimillion dollar business that makes commercial and industrial hinges. His objective was to assess how well the sixty-five employees fit into their current jobs. Like many companies, employees typically worked their way up through the ranks and landed in jobs that may or may not have been the best fit for their skills over all those years.

Kodrin, who has been at the company less than a year, spent his first six months performing his own assessments of the workers and then increasing accountability for everyone. "It was a person-by-person activity," says Kodrin. "Tenure gave them a certain entitlement." Many of the workers were familiar only with one aspect of the job, so Kodrin paired many to allow cross-training. "For the mid-level managers, if there's a weakness but the intent is good, I say 'I'll work with you.' I'll give them an example of what has worked so they get an idea of what we're looking for. Some, however, are just used to taking orders. I have two rules: treat everyone with respect, and tell the truth. Some of these people have not been introduced to new ideas in a long time."

You may be in the same position as Kodrin, the person responsible for finding the best job matches for people. Or, you might be in the same position as the managers and employees Kodrin found when he started, sitting in the same job for a lengthy period of time. You might find yourself in a position that is a total mismatch to your Executive Skills strengths or one that is a perfect fit.

Of what he found when he arrived, Kodrin says: "Many of the people had been in the same position or had been promoted to the next level of incompetence. Their myopic views had caused stagnation to the organization. Their mindset of doing the same thing over and over but expecting different results is the classic definition of insanity revisited over and over."

Any department or organization at any time could undertake an evaluation of how well people are matched to what they do. If you regularly benchmark your goodness of fit in the job and in the organization, you stand a much better chance of not being the one who is either downsized or reassigned. When you think about it, if you're perfectly matched for a job that the business values, you would hardly be the logical candidate for elimination or reassignment. This is why it's so critical to stay on top of how well your skills match to your position or job.

As we discussed in Chapter 6, while your skills strengths and weaknesses stay the same, jobs evolve, which could include yours. You have a great advantage if you realize that your job is evolving away from your Executive Skills strengths before your boss does. This gives you time to create a personal strategy to deal with it by making environmental changes, or trying to navigate yourself into a different position or situation that again plays to your strengths.

Outsourcing Your Weaknesses

Another part of your Executive Skills career strategy should be to consider which method you want to use to minimize your weaknesses so they don't get in the way. In other parts of the book, we discussed how to deal with your weaknesses, either by changing your behavior or changing the environment or task. At times, an easier approach is to pair with someone who has a strength that is one of your significant weaknesses. We refer to this as *outsourcing* your weakest Executive Skills. This very naturally happens in many relationships and marriages, though the couples may not have thought of it as outsourcing weaknesses to each other.

For example, if one partner is great at Working Memory and the other is not, then complicated driving directions should be handled by the one with the strong Working Memory, especially if there are screaming kids in the back seat and it's rush hour. Or, if one partner is very strong in Defining and Achieving Goals, then that person would be much better at orchestrating the next big vacation trip than the other partner. The same holds true at work.

Over time, you should be able to tell how successful you are at modifying your behavior or changing the environment to accommodate your weaknesses. You then will know how much effort it typically takes for you and perhaps those around you. Based on your success rate and amount of effort, you then can determine in which cases it would be easier to just find someone who complements your weaknesses. If it becomes obvious to you that your Executive Skills strengths and weaknesses are exact opposites to those of a close coworker, there's a great opportunity for the two of you to partner on those issues that may be caused by each of your respective weaknesses. You'll be in a position to help each other. Of course, presuming the other person is not as aware of the twelve cognitive brain functions known as Executive Skills, you'll have a slight education process ahead of you before you can outsource your weaknesses. (Unless, of course, you buy copies of this book for everyone you know!)

Knowing what you now know about Executive Skills and how they work, you also can take on someone else's weaknesses as long as they play directly to your strengths. This can place you in the position of internal hero. For example, if one of your greatest strengths is Time Management, you now can easily see who around you has that specific skill as one of their significant weaknesses. Even if you're not in a management position, you can take it upon yourself to get more things in the business to run on time by leveraging your strength. If you're high in Time Management and some around you are not, you might already have fallen into the role of keeping various things on time without realizing why. Besides not having had the knowledge of Executive Skills you now possess, you might not have realized it because it was hardly an effortful task for you, since it played to one of your key strengths.

If your superiors are somewhat observant, they will notice that you're volunteering to help with someone or something beyond the scope of your duties. This can be perceived as taking some personal initiative to improve those around you. You just may be identified as someone with potential leadership abilities. Of course, you always have to be on the lookout for external factors that could cause your Executive Skills to break down, a topic which we discuss in Chapter 8.

8

Reaching and Dealing with Cognitive Bandwidth

WHEN YOU'RE STRUGGLING with overload and feel like you're losing it, on the edge, not able to remember things, and totally stressed out, you may have reached the end of what we call your *cognitive bandwidth*. Whereas you have a built-in capacity to meet complex challenges and opportunities through the use of the functions of the prefrontal cortex of the brain, there can be times when literally too much information overloads the system. There's nothing necessarily wrong with you; it's just that the actual amount of information you're attempting to handle or process through the twelve brain functions has exceeded the capacity of those functions. This causes your frontal lobes to effectively break down.

Symptoms of such a breakdown could be feeling overwhelmed, having trouble planning your day, or having a feeling that there's so much to do you don't even know where to begin. You also might see it at home, such as finding yourself screaming at your children or spouse for something that at other times would be considered trivial. Exceeding cognitive bandwidth occurs when information load exceeds information capacity. Your Executive Skills, which are required to manage the information in the brain, just can't handle the volume, speed, or complexity, or a combination of all three. The information to which you have access can exceed your hardwired or cognitive ability to manage it.

We know from psychological and neuropsychological research that information overload degrades Executive Skills. And when your Executive Skills fail under pressure, your weakest skills fail first. When the amount of information coming in exceeds cognitive bandwidth, the result is that decision-making speed and accuracy can suffer and mistakes increase.

Fatigue also lowers your threshold as your weakest Executive Skills begin to fail, in which case you can also exceed your cognitive bandwidth. You can simply become too tired or exhausted from working too many long hours over a period of time or working long hours under nonstop pressure. You can probably remember a time when you simply felt too tired to make a logical or complex decision, so you put it off to another time. You might have had a breakdown in your Executive Skills due to fatigue.

Exceeding Cognitive Bandwidth

Exceeding your cognitive bandwidth can grow out of information overload, which happens because information is so freely flowing. Not all information has to be dealt with and much of it can passively be ignored. However, information overload can evolve into exceeding cognitive bandwidth when much of the information is relevant or you attempt to deal with most or all of it. Information is flowing at you nonstop, from e-mail, phone, cell phone, instant messages, and PDA. You can easily exceed cognitive bandwidth by treating all information you receive as of equal importance.

In a similar fashion, *stress* also has a detrimental effect on Executive Skills. Stress creates unnecessary "noise" or clutter in the brain's information-processing systems and decreases your capacity to manage information. Although Executive Skills such as Focus and Working

Memory are highly vulnerable to stress, we've noticed another significant effect: Stress is most likely to have a negative impact on your weakest skills. This means that the Executive Skills that already are a struggle for you will decline further when you're subjected to too much information or increased stress.

This decline in a skill can actually serve as a barometer, indicating that you're overloaded or experiencing excessive stress. For example, if you're already weak in Organization and start to feel even more disorganized, or look that way to others, this is often a sign that you're trying to handle too many demands or are overly stressed. Or if you're low in Flexibility and Emotion Control and begin to feel or show increased frustration, irritability, or even anger, this can be a signal that you're overloaded.

When you exceed your cognitive bandwidth, logical decisions cannot be made, since Executives Skills are needed to execute. Without them, you will not be able to prioritize, manage emotions, deal with the bigger picture, and function effectively.

When your Executive Skills are not working well due to exceeding your cognitive bandwidth, you're experiencing what is called Executive Skills dysfunction. The good news is that your cognitive bandwidth can be increased by increasing efficiency. Interestingly, young adults who have grown up processing multiple streams of information simultaneously in many ways already may be more adept at handling more simultaneous information, since they have developed those skills naturally throughout their youth. However, even they have limitations in their cognitive bandwidth. How much information you can process before reaching the end of your cognitive bandwidth will be obvious to you, as well as to those around you when it happens.

The key step to avoid reaching maximum cognitive bandwidth is to select and prioritize information. Critical to this selection process is establishing priorities for types of information, so that not all information is viewed as being equal. You have to essentially turn off some sources of information or at least ignore some.

Stress at Work

Exceeding cognitive bandwidth is a very real thing in business today, and there's no shortage of stress as a result. Four out of five managers and executives are stressed at work, with a third being highly stressed (see Survey 8-1). Slightly more managers than executives are stressed, with the leading causes for both being deadlines, interruptions, conflicting responsibilities, expectations, and e-mail overload.

Ironically, Executive Skills are needed for decision making and the more stressed you are the less you can do it. This also could explain why many companies hire consultants and consulting firms to help create strategies and direction. Many in the business become so consumed by executing and driven by deadlines and the need to make the numbers that there is little free time left to just think. As a result, companies are essentially outsourcing thinking. And outside consultants tend to bring an unencumbered perspective, since they're not consumed by the day-to-day activities of the business itself.

SURVEY 8-1: Stress at Work
When it comes to my stress level at work, I feel:

Highly stressed	29%
Moderately stressed	51%
Slightly stressed	20%
Not at all stressed	1%

The primary causes of stress facing me are:

Deadlines	52%
Interruptions	42%
Conflicting responsibilities	37%
Expectations	35%
E-mail overload	35%
Deliverables	34%
Budget constraints	34%
Customer demands	34%
Lack of down time	30%
Staffing	30%
Number of hours worked	28%
Information overload	27%
Conflict	26%
Meetings	26%

Pressure from above	23%
Finishing something	20%
Making the numbers	17%
Personal/family issues	16%
Criticism	11%

When it comes to my stress level at work, I feel:

	Senior Executive	Manager
Highly stressed	26%	32%
Moderately stressed	49%	52%
Slightly stressed	24%	16%
Not at all stressed	1%	0%

VOICES FROM THE FRONT LINES
Stress at Work

"Stress is now greater than I can remember in my 30 years of work history."

■

"The biggest cause of stress is the unrealistic expectations in the volume of work that is expected. The second is the amount of time that is expected. Not that long ago extra time at the office would get you ahead, now extra time is needed just to keep your head."

■

"The demands and pressures seem to be greater the longer a person is with the company. It becomes as though they think of you as a machine with no life and no feelings. And down time? If there is down time it means we have too much staff and need to eliminate positions and distribute more work to remaining staff."

■

"The 40-hour work week is a myth anymore for most managers. It is an expected 50–60 hours to get the job done and a large number of things still don't get completed because of unrealistic expectations. We are still human beings who can only do so much in a day."

■

"I just had yet another round of conversations with some executives. One of the main stresses we all feel is too much to do and declining resources needed to get the job done. Fewer employees, means more responsibility and less time to focus on any one thing."

■

"My biggest stress is not being able to have time to really fix anything at root cause because of the diversions to firefight, yet being expected to fix everything quickly without buy-in, assigned resources or proper funding."

■

"Unrealistic expectations and deadlines may result in a very unproductive work environment. Worst of all, reading e-mails, attending meetings and managing interruptions may not improve customer service or enhance customer's experience with our products/services."

E-Mail Overload

One of the leading causes of exceeding cognitive bandwidth is the volume of e-mail you have to deal with on a daily basis. With the majority of managers and executives spending between one and two hours a day on e-mail, and a third spending three hours or more a day, there's no break from the constant information flow (see Survey 8-2). Based on research, e-mail overload has gotten so bad that the majority of business leaders delete e-mail without even reading it.

Much of the e-mail received is unnecessary. "Junk mail is junk mail—whether it's in the post box on the end of my lane, or the in-box on my computers," says one survey respondent. Says another: "If folks could only get two basic rules: don't cc the world, and if someone should fall out of the loop, take them off the list and do not hit reply-all on general stuff. And if folks would stop with the unnecessary forwarding of jokes and stupid stuff and chain letters and political requests, we'd live in a better world."

To decrease the chance of hitting your cognitive bandwidth requires controlling the amount of e-mail information you receive. When you feel totally overwhelmed and your Executive Skills start failing, it is a good idea to back off of e-mail, as a very quick fix. "Our CEO introduced e-mail free Fridays so we can talk to each other again," says one manager. In addition to curtailing the flow of information to give you time to breathe and give your frontal lobes a chance to recharge, you will likely pick up a significant amount of time on a daily basis.

Other than by corporate directive, the most logical way to cut back on e-mail is in your hands. "It's a sign of the times: I can't function without e-mail or a cell phone anymore," says one manager. "Self-discipline is the only way to manage my business communications." Without such self-discipline, e-mail can add to your hitting your cognitive bandwidth limits, in which case something else will have to give to let you regroup.

SURVEY 8-2: E-Mail Management

How much time daily do you spend sending/receiving/reading/writing e-mail?

Less than 15 minutes	1%
16 to 30 minutes	3%
31 to 60 minutes	16%
1 to 2 hours	50%
3 to 4 hours	25%
More than 4 hours	6%

How much of the e-mail you receive do you personally deem unnecessary?

76% to 100%	4%
51% to 75%	30%
26% to 50%	45%
0% to 25%	22%

How do you deal with e-mail overload?

Deleting without reading	60%
Reading only from known sources	47%
Using filtering software	45%
Reading at certain times	45%

Viewing without opening	40%
Sending fewer CCs	26%
Using multiple accounts	16%
Eliminating internal copies	15%
Receiving fewer CC's	10%
Ignoring much of/all e-mail	8%
Having someone else read	4%
No longer using e-mail	0%

VOICES FROM THE FRONT LINES
E-Mail

"E-mail started as a better way to communicate. It has evolved into an albatross."

■

"E-mail is the great cop-out to critical thinking and reasoned management. It wastes as much time as it saves. E-mail is often just a CYA tool, particularly when there is a bare copy without explaining why people are copied."

■

"It is not just company e-mail. It is the personal e-mail, too, that continues to complicate e-mail overload."

■

"When it gets out of control (e.g., post vacation) I have a ruthless flow chart that I follow to get it back under control. E-mail is so pervasive we do not think to teach people how to use it well—all organizations should do this. Perhaps even schools should do it. People confuse the speed of transmission of e-mail (good!) with speed of production of the original material (bad!). Any written material more than a few lines benefits from drafting, contemplation, revision (perhaps several times) and the sending. If this were done more and better the volume of e-mail would probably reduce as well since less superfluous activity would be generated."

Working Too Many Hours

Another reason you can exceed your cognitive bandwidth is due to fatigue caused by work overload. Businesspeople today are faced with heavy workloads, resulting in many long days at the office and even a lot of work done at home and on weekends. The majority of executives and managers now spend ten hours or more a day working on a typical workday (see Survey 8-3). For them, the 40-hour workweek is only a memory, with 58 percent working 51 hours or more a week.

Working long days tends to increase fatigue, which leads to the failings of your weakest Executive Skills. As your skills start to fail, you tend to pursue working more hours, since your daily goals are not being accomplished. This leads to more hours, causing more failure of Executive Skills, and the cycle continues until you exceed your cognitive bandwidth. At that point, you need a break, since your Executive Skills will be ineffective.

We know from our research that most businesspeople are most productive before 9 A.M. and after 5 P.M., as people try to avoid interruptions. However, once people figured out that this was the best time to get access to the boss, they started to also come in during those high-productivity times. We also have found that people at work are least productive between 11 A.M. and 2 P.M. Use your lunch time to recharge yourself so that you have plenty of cognitive bandwidth left. Taking a walk, taking someone to lunch, exercising, and practicing relaxation techniques are great ways to give yourself time to rejuvenate your cognitive bandwidth.

SURVEY 8-3: Work Time

On a typical workday, the number of hours I work (office, home, etc.) is about:

6 hours or less	1%
7 hours	3%
8 hours	11%
9 hours	27%
10 hours	32%
11 hours	14%
12 hours	9%
13 hours or more	3%

In a typical workweek, the number of hours I work (office, home, etc.) is about:

30 hours or less	1%
31–40 hours	8%
41–50 hours	34%
51–60 hours	40%
61–70 hours	15%
71 hours or more	3%

VOICES FROM THE FRONT LINES
Work Time

"Gone are the days of the 40-hour work week. My company expects all managers to put in 50 to 60 hours a week as the average."

■

"I feel I am compelled to be in the office for more hours than necessary just because it is expected. I feel that if people spent only 6 to 7 hours in the office a day, 5 days a week we would all become more productive and more would get done. Too much time is spent chit-chatting and talking. Work has become too many people's lives; they live to work instead of work to live."

■

"With my Blackberry and cell phone with me, anytime I am out of the office (vacations, dinner table, etc.) my wife and other family members might argue that I work 24/7."

■

"Fifty hours is a typical minimum workweek for most of the managers/executives I know. This likely doesn't include them doing e-mails at home, answering Blackberries at family events, etc. It is a bit out of control in that regard."

Identifying Outside Forces

There are several outside factors that cause stress and strain on your cognitive bandwidth. For example, constant interruptions coupled with never-ending information streams can increase pressure, at which time your weakest Executive Skills will start to fail, followed by the others. "Constant interruptions are the hardest thing to deal with," says Ralph

Menzano, North American director of transportation for Oracle. And interruptions at work today are constant and come from multiple directions simultaneously.

Additionally, different pieces of information come from multiple directions at multiple times so it's no longer a cohesive message that can be stored and referred to in one place. "I don't handle e-mail the way I used to," says Menzano. "Using a Blackberry has forced me to handle e-mail twice. You may need to file it away later, say, using a mail folder, when you get to your computer. I've had to give up how I used to handle everyday items. For example, I used to keep comprehensive histories of projects but now I can't. There are too many pieces of information in voicemail, text messages, instant messages and e-mail—it all adds to my stress. To me, it is added stress because we now have fragmented documentation for projects, cases, or events."

Compounding information overload is the fragmentation of information into or from different forms. "No one is disciplined enough to manage it," says Menzano, who considers himself moderately stressed. "When I get a piece of information I instinctively want to figure out how to file it. I'm too detail-oriented to discard anything, so I keep it in forms such as saved voicemails or general e-mail in-boxes. It's about the equivalent of a pack rat. It's like having a desk full of papers that can't be discarded easily because they need to be saved for future filing."

Capacity and Executive Skills are diminished when the outside forces, singly or in combinations, become too great.

Dealing with Outside Forces

There are specific actions you can take to keep outside forces under control. If you don't, you have a chance of being overtaken by them, causing you to exceed your cognitive bandwidth, at which time your Executive Skills will break down.

■ *Deadlines.* This is the top cause of stress for the majority of managers. If the deadlines come and go, you can be OK since there will be time to recharge between them. If they're steady, you won't get out from under them, which eventually will overload your Executive Skills. You need to take steps to either get breaks between deadlines or vary them with other low-effort tasks.

- *Interruptions.* You can attempt to schedule the interruptions, as much as possible so that they, in general, are only either encouraged or allowed at certain times. For example, closing your door, if you have one, a few times a day can be a deterrent to those around you. You also can set a filter or barrier to interruptions, such as having certain requests go to someone else first. Keep in mind that sometimes you might be unconsciously allowing or even encouraging interruptions to get out of an effortful task.

- *Conflicting Responsibilities.* If you're weak in Planning and Prioritization it's even more critical that you prioritize. If a superior is not being clear or there are mixed messages from various people, take it upon yourself to get the message either clarified or at least synchronized. Otherwise, you'll never complete what is expected, causing frustration, and possibly cognitive bandwidth failure due to high stress.

- *Expectations.* These sometimes need to be scaled back or at least made realistic. When it comes to requiring results, 40 percent of managers say that top management is extremely demanding, but only 22 percent rank those demands as being extremely realistic, based on our research. Expectations need to be negotiated with both parties agreeing on what is expected and on what time and resources will be needed. Constant communication back and forth about the status of the task or project should follow.

- *E-Mail Overload.* Some of this overload can be resolved by filtering, either using technology or assistants. Key to managing e-mail is prioritization, so that critical issues are addressed first. In some cases, having a separate, private e-mail address for *really* important matters can help. If you're an executive or manager, you can give your staff permission not to have to instantly respond to every e-mail, which can cause constant interruptions throughout the day.

- *Deliverables/Production.* Reports, projects, updates, presentations, and budgets fall into this category. These generally come and go, so if you can get through the one at hand you then can move to a potentially low effortful task. If deliverables are constant over a lengthy period of time, you likely will hit your cognitive bandwidth limit.

▪ *Budget Constraints*. In general, everyone faces some budget limitation. This requires prioritization, since you can only do what you can do. Trying to do more than your Executive Skills can handle for a lengthy period of time will cause them to fail.

▪ *Customer Demands*. It's no secret that customers today are more demanding. If you're low in Self-Restraint, you might tend to promise them more than can be delivered. It's best to clarify what you'll deliver and then set and manage expectations from there so there are no surprises.

▪ *Lack of Down Time*. The obvious: Take a rest. The least productive times of the day are between 11 A.M. and 2 P.M., so that could be a good time for a breather. Switching to a less effortful task also could help. Try to schedule down time in advance, such as a break in the middle of the day or after completing a high-effort task.

▪ *Staffing*. Use your Executive Skills knowledge of strengths and weaknesses to navigate yourself and those you manage into better fitting jobs or tasks. If there's not enough staffing, it means more prioritizing has to be used to focus on what really needs to get done.

▪ *Number of Hours Worked*. With 85 percent of senior executives and managers working at least 9-hour workdays, and with a quarter working 11 hours or more, there can be plenty of opportunity to wear down your Executive Skills and hit the cognitive bandwidth ceiling. However, by better matching jobs with people based on Executive Skills strengths, work can take less time with tasks being of lower effort for those doing them.

▪ *Information Overload*. With so much information coming at you from so many sources, it is essential to establish systems to prioritize the information. Quickly sift through and set up filters, using technology or people.

▪ *Conflict*. There are two ways to deal with conflict. The first is to deal with it head on, and get it resolved one way or another. The second is to reframe the conflict in your mind so that it doesn't matter. Either of these solutions is fine, so use whichever is most appropriate to the situation. For example, if a colleague outside your department is bothered by a department-wide decision you have made but is not personally affected, you might best handle the conflict by simply ignoring it.

▪ *Meetings.* People aren't likely to claim they don't have enough meetings to attend. If you can't reduce the number of meetings you attend, try to make sure that that the meetings you do attend become more efficient by matching the Executive Skills of the people at the meeting to what is needed at that meeting. Also, precise agendas with proper time allocation can help. A person who could help this happen would be high in the skills of Prioritization, Organization, and Time Management.

▪ *Pressure from Above.* Require more clarity in communication to properly set achievable expectations as well as priorities. It would be easier to deal with this pressure if you're high in Emotion Control and Planning/Prioritization.

▪ *Workload.* The sheer volume of work, at times daunting, needs to be either diminished or spread out. If too much work is being crammed into too short a period of time on a continual basis, cognitive bandwidth will be exceeded and you won't be efficient or effective doing *any* of the work.

▪ *Finishing Something.* Prioritize what needs to get done first. While 95 percent of executives and managers make daily lists, 99 percent do not get everything on it done by the end of the day. Some things at the bottom of the list have no chance of ever being addressed. Just remove them from the list or get agreement from your boss that they'll never realistically be done, given all the other pressing issues of the day.

▪ *Making the Numbers.* Do whatever it takes for you or your department or company to make the numbers, and eliminate whatever gets in the way, especially if you're low in Focus.

▪ *Personal/Family Issues.* Some issues, such as financial problems or a serious family illness, can weigh you down. The best way to handle such situations is to compartmentalize. Acknowledge to yourself that there's nothing you can do about it right now while at work. Also, talk to someone else about it. And most importantly, get enough sleep, since fatigue will only cause your Executive Skills weaknesses to degrade more, potentially causing a dangerous downward spiral.

■ *Criticism.* If it is directional conflict, such as your boss asking you to do something differently, then you have to deal with it and attempt to correct it. If it's criticism from someone who has no direct bearing on you or what you do, then just ignore it and move on.

You're less likely to move up in an organization if you continually exceed your cognitive bandwidth. If you experience Executive Skills dysfunction on a regular basis, it will not be a secret, since your sense of falling apart will be obvious to others. You might find yourself snapping at coworkers or losing your cool for something trivial or maybe for no reason at all. You probably can think of someone at work who has acted like this in the past. Seemingly normal most days and then on one day, the person just blows up for no apparent reason, perhaps finally exceeding their cognitive bandwidth. The reasons may not be immediately obvious to you, since that person's weakest Executive Skills that gave out may be so different from your weaknesses that it does not seem logical at first glance. That person could have been dealing with one-too-many high-effort tasks, with no breaks between.

The degree to which your Executive Skills are taxed can also depend on what kind of a department or organization you work in: the looser the structure, the more the demands on Executive Skills; the more rigid the structure, the fewer demands. This is because in a looser environment you have to use your skills more frequently. In a more rigid environment, rules and processes dictate many actions. For example, an executive who attends many meetings a day can be kept on time by an efficient assistant, although the executive may be low in Time Management.

One example of a looser structure would be working at home, where increased independence means using more Executive Skills more frequently, and where having certain skill strengths can make it much easier to succeed. For example, Task Initiation, Time Management, and Focus are self-discipline skills, which would be of high use when working alone or in a home office. They also would be great strengths to have in a start-up or entrepreneurial environment.

The Final Frontier

Using your knowledge of Executive Skills strategies and tactics can help improve your life at work. The more people who learn about Executive Skills, the better the chances will be that more people will end up in the right positions. This could be a big win for you as well as for the organization for which you work. By understanding your strengths and weaknesses and seeing the implications, you can direct your path into goodness of fit situations. You now know how to identify your strengths and weaknesses, as well as the strengths and weaknesses of those around you. You know that playing to your strengths is always the best plan but that, at times, you will have to deal with your weaknesses.

But you now have the tools to do that. You can perhaps now understand why many work situations are the way they are and why you behaved the way you did in certain situations. You also will likely view those around you in a different light, identifying when one of their Executive Skills shines or fails.

Your new Executive Skills knowledge can serve you well, as you become much more aware of how your strengths and weaknesses play out in various circumstances. And when you find yourself in that perfect fit—the job in which you soar while people around you wonder how you do it, you can feel comfortable knowing that you're successfully using all that you have: You're using your Smarts.

About NFI Research

EVERY TWO WEEKS, NFI Research sends surveys via e-mail to 2,000 executives and managers in fifty countries. The surveys are short and results are anonymous. When the questions list potential answers, NFI Research asks respondents to check all answers that apply, thereby providing a majority consensus in results. The surveys do not necessarily match intensity of feeling about any given subject, but rather what most respondents agree and disagree on. NFI Research repeats some surveys over the years, so that benchmarking is possible and changes in attitude are identified. NFI does not share the e-mail addresses or any personal information about any of its members. There is no charge for membership, and the members all receive the survey results every other week for free. Response rates are always at least 10 percent or higher. NFI

Research survey results are routinely reported in newspapers, magazines, and newsletters around the world.

Survey participants fall into one of two categories: *senior executives* (chief executive officer, chairman, president, chief operating officer, chief financial officer, chief information officer, executive vice president, senior vice president, general manager, etc.) or *managers* (assistant vice president, director, manager, supervisor, etc.). Respondents are usually split 50-50 between senior executives and managers. Some percentages do not equal 100 percent due to rounding. All research in this book, unless otherwise stated, is primary research conducted by NFI Research.

Respondents also identify themselves by company size, based on total number of employees, and the results generally are fairly evenly split among the groups. Some of those differences, as well as those between senior executives and managers, are illustrated in this book when the differences are worth noting. Company sizes are based on number of employees:

Small: Fewer than 499 employees

Medium: 500 to 9,999 employees

Large: 10,000 or more employees

A small sampling of the more than 1,000 companies for which members work are IBM, GE, Morgan Stanley, Microsoft, CIGNA, Fidelity, Merck, Motorola, Freddie Mac, Progressive, Travelers, Deloitte & Touche, MasterCard, Sears Roebuck, SAP, Oracle, Sony, Marriott International, Mercer, American Gas, Heineken, Western Energy Institute, Wal-Mart, Wells Fargo, ABN AMRO Bank, Air Canada, Agilent Technologies, Allied Waste Industries, American Association of Advertising Agencies, American Cancer Society, American Express, Apple Computer, 3M Company, AT&T, Bank of America, Bell Canada, Bell South, Best Buy, Circuit City, California Credit Union League, Bristol-Meyers Squibb Company, Canon, Cendant, Delta Air Lines, Unilever, and Procter and Gamble.

You may obtain further information at **www.nfiresearch.com,** where, if you are a senior executive or manager, you may apply for free membership. You may also contact the author directly at **chuck@nfire search.com.**

Executive Skills Assessments and Questionnaires

1. Executive Skills Profile: Self

Read each item in the questionnaire below and then rate the item based on the extent to which you agree or disagree with how well it describes you. Use the five-point scoring system to choose the appropriate score. Adding the five scores for each item gives you your total score for that Executive Skill.

	Strongly Disagree	Somewhat Disagree	Neither Agree nor Disagree	Somewhat Agree	Strongly Agree
1. I take my time before making up my mind	1	2	3	4	5
2. I see myself as tactful and diplomatic	1	2	3	4	5
3. I think before I speak	1	2	3	4	5
4. I make sure I have all the facts before I take action	1	2	3	4	5
5. I seldom make comments that make people uncomfortable	1	2	3	4	5

Total Score _____

	Strongly Disagree	Somewhat Disagree	Neither Agree nor Disagree	Somewhat Agree	Strongly Agree
6. I have a good memory for facts, dates, and details	1	2	3	4	5
7. I am good at remembering the things that I have committed to do	1	2	3	4	5
8. I very naturally remember to complete tasks	1	2	3	4	5
9. I keep sight of goals that I want to accomplish	1	2	3	4	5
10. When I'm busy, I keep track of both the big picture and the details	1	2	3	4	5

Total Score _____

	Strongly Disagree	Somewhat Disagree	Neither Agree nor Disagree	Somewhat Agree	Strongly Agree
11. I can keep my emotions in check when on the job	1	2	3	4	5
12. I usually handle confrontations calmly	1	2	3	4	5
13. Little things don't affect me emotionally and distract me from the task at hand	1	2	3	4	5
14. When frustrated or angry, I keep my cool	1	2	3	4	5
15. I easily defer my personal feelings until after a task has been completed	1	2	3	4	5

Total Score _____

	Strongly Disagree	Somewhat Disagree	Neither Agree nor Disagree	Somewhat Agree	Strongly Agree
16. When I have a job to do or task to finish I easily avoid distractions	1	2	3	4	5
17. Once I start an assignment, I work diligently until it is completed	1	2	3	4	5
18. I find it easy to stay focused on my work	1	2	3	4	5
19. Even when interrupted, I get back to work to complete the job at hand	1	2	3	4	5
20. I attend to a task even when I find it somewhat tedious	1	2	3	4	5

Total Score _____

	Strongly Disagree	Somewhat Disagree	Neither Agree nor Disagree	Somewhat Agree	Strongly Agree
21. Once I've been given a job or task, I like to start it immediately	1	2	3	4	5
22. Procrastination is usually not a problem for me	1	2	3	4	5
23. No matter what the task, I believe in getting started as soon as possible	1	2	3	4	5
24. I can get right to work even if there's something I'd rather be doing	1	2	3	4	5
25. I generally start tasks early	1	2	3	4	5

Total Score _____

	Strongly Disagree	Somewhat Disagree	Neither Agree nor Disagree	Somewhat Agree	Strongly Agree
26. When I start my day, I have a clear plan in mind for what I hope to accomplish	1	2	3	4	5
27. When I have a lot to do, I focus on the most important things	1	2	3	4	5
28. I have formulated plans to achieve my most important long-term goals	1	2	3	4	5
29. I am good at identifying priorities and sticking to them	1	2	3	4	5
30. I typically break big tasks down into subtasks and timelines	1	2	3	4	5

Total Score _____

	Strongly Disagree	Somewhat Disagree	Neither Agree nor Disagree	Somewhat Agree	Strongly Agree
31. I am an organized person	1	2	3	4	5
32. I am good at maintaining systems for organizing my work	1	2	3	4	5
33. It is natural for me to keep my work area neat and organized	1	2	3	4	5
34. It's easy for me to keep track of my materials	1	2	3	4	5
35. It is easy for me to organize things, such as e-mail, inbox, and to-do items	1	2	3	4	5

Total Score _____

	Strongly Disagree	Somewhat Disagree	Neither Agree nor Disagree	Somewhat Agree	Strongly Agree
36. I pace myself according to the time demands of a task	1	2	3	4	5
37. At the end of the day, I've usually finished what I set out to do	1	2	3	4	5
38. I am good at estimating how long it takes to do something	1	2	3	4	5
39. I am usually on time for appointments and activities	1	2	3	4	5
40. I routinely set and follow a daily schedule of activities	1	2	3	4	5

Total Score _____

	Strongly Disagree	Somewhat Disagree	Neither Agree nor Disagree	Somewhat Agree	Strongly Agree
41. When I encounter an obstacle, I still achieve my goal	1	2	3	4	5
42. I think of myself as being driven to meet my goals	1	2	3	4	5
43. I am good at setting and achieving high levels of performance	1	2	3	4	5
44. I have good ability to set long-term goals	1	2	3	4	5
45. I easily give up immediate pleasures while working on long-term goals	1	2	3	4	5

Total Score _____

	Strongly Disagree	Somewhat Disagree	Neither Agree nor Disagree	Somewhat Agree	Strongly Agree
46. I consider myself to be flexible and adaptive to change	1	2	3	4	5
47. I generally see different ways to address or attack a problem	1	2	3	4	5
48. I take unexpected events in stride	1	2	3	4	5
49. I easily can view situations from the perspective of other people	1	2	3	4	5
50. I think well on my feet	1	2	3	4	5

Total Score _____

	Strongly Disagree	Somewhat Disagree	Neither Agree nor Disagree	Somewhat Agree	Strongly Agree
51. I easily recognize when a task is a good match for my skills and abilities	1	2	3	4	5
52. I routinely evaluate my performance and devise methods for personal improvement	1	2	3	4	5
53. I generally step back from a situation in order to make objective decisions	1	2	3	4	5
54. I enjoy strategic thinking and sound problem solving	1	2	3	4	5
55. I can review a situation and see where I could have done things differently	1	2	3	4	5

Total Score _____

	Strongly Disagree	Somewhat Disagree	Neither Agree nor Disagree	Somewhat Agree	Strongly Agree
56. I enjoy working in a highly demanding, fast-paced environment	1	2	3	4	5
57. Pressure helps me perform at my best	1	2	3	4	5
58. Jobs that include a fair degree of unpredictability appeal to me	1	2	3	4	5
59. I am comfortable taking risks when the situation calls for it	1	2	3	4	5
60. I like jobs where there are not many set schedules	1	2	3	4	5

Total Score _____

After you've answered all the questions, go back and find your two or three highest and the two or three lowest scores and enter them opposite the appropriate skill listed on the next page. Those will be your strongest and weakest Executive Skills.

SCORE CHART: Self-Asessment

Items	Executive Skill	Scores
1–5	Self-Restraint	————
6–10	Working Memory	————
11–15	Emotion Control	————
16–20	Focus	————
21–25	Task Initiation	————
26–30	Planning/Prioritization	————
31–35	Organization	————
36–40	Time Management	————
41–45	Defining and Achieving Goals	————
46–50	Flexibility	————
51–55	Observation	————
56–60	Stress Tolerance	————

2. Executive Skills Profile: Job or Task

This questionnaire enables you to rank the Executive Skills that are needed for a job, task, or project. First, be precise about what you are measuring. For example, you can benchmark your entire job, or simply one aspect of it, such as your role in a project on which you're a team member. Write the job or task description in the space below.

_____

_____

_____

Which of the 12 Executive Skills listed below does the task or job require? Use the following assessment to rank which Executive Skills are required for the particular job or task identified above. Place a check mark next to the three executive skills most important to the job or task you identified above.

Job or Task Skills Required

Self-Restraint _____
> This is the ability to think before you act. It is the ability to resist the urge to say or do something to allow the time to evaluate the situation and how a behavior might affect it.

Working Memory _____
> This is the ability to hold information in memory while performing complex tasks and involves drawing on past learning or experience to apply to the situation at hand or to project into the future.

Emotion Control _____
> This is the ability to manage emotions in order to achieve goals, complete tasks, or control and direct behavior.

Focus _____
> This is the capacity to maintain attention to a situation or task in spite of distractions, fatigue, or boredom.

Task Initiation _____

This is the ability to begin projects or tasks without undue procrastination.

Planning/Prioritization _____

This is the capacity to develop a road map to arrive at a destination or goal, knowing which are the most important signposts along the way.

Organization _____

This is the ability to arrange or place according to a system.

Time Management _____

This is the capacity to estimate how much time one has, to allocate it effectively, and to stay within time limits and deadlines. It involves a sense that time is important.

Defining and Achieving Goals _____

This is the capacity to have a goal, follow through to the completion of the goal, and not be put off or distracted by competing interests.

Flexibility _____

This is the ability to revise plans in the face of obstacles, setbacks, new information, or mistakes. It relates to adaptability to changing conditions.

Observation _____

This is the capacity to stand back and take a birds-eye view of yourself in a situation and understand and make changes in the ways that you solve problems.

Stress Tolerance _____

This is the ability to thrive in stressful situations and to cope with uncertainty, change, and performance demands.

Self-Restraint _____

This is the ability to think before you act. It is the ability to resist the urge to say or do something to allow the time to evaluate the situation and how a behavior might impact it.

3. Executive Skills Profile: Others

This assessment allows you to determine the strengths and weaknesses of a colleague, subordinate, or boss. Read each item below and then rate the item based on the extent to which you agree or disagree with how well it describes the person you are evaluating. Use the five-point scoring system to choose the appropriate score. Adding the five scores for each item gives you your total score for that person's Executive Skill.

Person being evaluated: _____

	Strongly Disagree	Somewhat Disagree	Neither Agree nor Disagree	Somewhat Agree	Strongly Agree
1. They take their time before making up their mind	1	2	3	4	5
2. They see themselves as tactful and diplomatic	1	2	3	4	5
3. They think before they speak	1	2	3	4	5
4. They make sure they have all the facts before they take action	1	2	3	4	5
5. They seldom make comments that make people uncomfortable	1	2	3	4	5

Total Score _____

	Strongly Disagree	Somewhat Disagree	Neither Agree nor Disagree	Somewhat Agree	Strongly Agree
6. They have a good memory for facts, dates, and details	1	2	3	4	5
7. They are good at remembering the things that they have committed to do	1	2	3	4	5
8. They remember to complete tasks	1	2	3	4	5
9. They keep sight of goals that they want to accomplish	1	2	3	4	5
10. When they are busy, they keep track of both the big picture and the details	1	2	3	4	5

Total Score _____

	Strongly Disagree	Somewhat Disagree	Neither Agree nor Disagree	Somewhat Agree	Strongly Agree
11. They keep their emotions in check when on the job	1	2	3	4	5
12. They usually handle confrontations calmly	1	2	3	4	5
13. Little things don't affect them emotionally and distract them from the task at hand	1	2	3	4	5
14. When frustrated or angry, they keep their cool	1	2	3	4	5
15. They defer their personal feelings until after a task has been completed	1	2	3	4	5

Total Score _____

	Strongly Disagree	Somewhat Disagree	Neither Agree nor Disagree	Somewhat Agree	Strongly Agree
16. When they have a job to do or task to finish they easily avoid distractions	1	2	3	4	5
17. Once they start an assignment, they work diligently until it is completed	1	2	3	4	5
18. They stay focused on their work	1	2	3	4	5
19. Even when interrupted, they get back to work to complete the job at hand	1	2	3	4	5
20. They attend to a task even when they find it somewhat tedious	1	2	3	4	5

Total Score _____

	Strongly Disagree	Somewhat Disagree	Neither Agree nor Disagree	Somewhat Agree	Strongly Agree
21. Once they've been given a job or task, they start it immediately	1	2	3	4	5
22. Procrastination is usually not a problem for them	1	2	3	4	5
23. No matter what the task, they get started as soon as possible	1	2	3	4	5
24. They get right to work even if there's something they'd rather be doing	1	2	3	4	5
25. They start early as the best way to accomplish a task	1	2	3	4	5

Total Score _____

	Strongly Disagree	Somewhat Disagree	Neither Agree nor Disagree	Somewhat Agree	Strongly Agree
26. When they start their day, they have a clear plan in mind for what they hope to accomplish	1	2	3	4	5
27. When they have a lot to do, they can focus on the most important things	1	2	3	4	5
28. They have formulated plans to achieve their most important long-term goals	1	2	3	4	5
29. They are good at identifying priorities and sticking to them	1	2	3	4	5
30. They typically break big tasks down into sub-tasks and timelines	1	2	3	4	5

Total Score _____

	Strongly Disagree	Somewhat Disagree	Neither Agree nor Disagree	Somewhat Agree	Strongly Agree
31. They are well organized	1	2	3	4	5
32. They are good at maintaining systems for organizing their work	1	2	3	4	5
33. Their work area is neat and organized	1	2	3	4	5
34. They keep track of their materials	1	2	3	4	5
35. They always organize things, such as e-mail, in-box, and to-do items	1	2	3	4	5

Total Score _____

	Strongly Disagree	Somewhat Disagree	Neither Agree nor Disagree	Somewhat Agree	Strongly Agree
36. They pace themselves according to the time demands of a task	1	2	3	4	5
37. At the end of the day, they have usually finished what they set out to do	1	2	3	4	5
38. They are good at estimating how long it takes to do something	1	2	3	4	5
39. They are usually on time for appointments and activities	1	2	3	4	5
40. They routinely set and follow a daily schedule of activities	1	2	3	4	5

Total Score _____

	Strongly Disagree	Somewhat Disagree	Neither Agree nor Disagree	Somewhat Agree	Strongly Agree
41. When they encounter an obstacle, they still achieve their goal	1	2	3	4	5
42. They are driven to meet their goals	1	2	3	4	5
43. They are good at setting and achieving high levels of performance	1	2	3	4	5
44. They have good ability to set long-term goals	1	2	3	4	5
45. They easily give up immediate pleasures while working on long-term goals	1	2	3	4	5

Total Score _____

	Strongly Disagree	Somewhat Disagree	Neither Agree nor Disagree	Somewhat Agree	Strongly Agree
46. They are flexible and adapt well to change	1	2	3	4	5
47. They generally see different ways to address or attack a problem	1	2	3	4	5
48. They take unexpected events in stride	1	2	3	4	5
49. They easily can view situations from the perspective of other people	1	2	3	4	5
50. They think well on their feet	1	2	3	4	5

Total Score _____

	Strongly Disagree	Somewhat Disagree	Neither Agree nor Disagree	Somewhat Agree	Strongly Agree
51. They easily recognize when a task is a good match for their skills and abilities	1	2	3	4	5
52. They routinely evaluate their performance and devise methods for personal improvement	1	2	3	4	5
53. They generally step back from a situation in order to make objective decisions	1	2	3	4	5
54. They enjoy strategic thinking and sound problem solving	1	2	3	4	5
55. They can review a situation and see where they could have done things differently	1	2	3	4	5

Total Score _____

	Strongly Disagree	Somewhat Disagree	Neither Agree nor Disagree	Somewhat Agree	Strongly Agree
56. They enjoy working in a highly demanding, fast-paced environment	1	2	3	4	5
57. Pressure helps them perform at their best	1	2	3	4	5
58. Jobs that include a fair degree of unpredictability appeal to them	1	2	3	4	5
59. They are comfortable taking risks when the situation calls for it	1	2	3	4	5
60. They like jobs where there are not many set schedules	1	2	3	4	5

Total Score _____

SCORE CHART: Assessment of Others

Items	Executive Skill	Scores
1–5	Self-Restraint	_____
6–10	Working Memory	_____
11–15	Emotion Control	_____
16–20	Focus	_____
21–25	Task Initiation	_____
26–30	Planning/Prioritization	_____
31–35	Organization	_____
36–40	Time Management	_____
41–45	Defining and Achieving Goals	_____
46–50	Flexibility	_____
51–55	Observation	_____
56–60	Stress Tolerance	_____

4. Matching Executive Skills, Job Skills, and Skills Most Valued by Organization

How do your skills and those required for the job compare to what is most valued by your organization? In the worksheet on the next page, assess how your skills and those required for the job compare to what is most valued by your business. In the first column, simply mark your three highest and lowest Executive Skills (from the self-assessment questions in Chapter 1). In the second column, mark the skills required for your job or task from Questionnaire 6-1 in Chapter 6 (Executive Skills Required for Job or Task). In the third column, mark what your organization values.

You now can assess the alignment among your Executive Skills, those skills required for your job or task, and those skills valued by the organization for which you work.

	Your Executive Skills Level	Executive Skills Required for Job or Task	Executive Skills Truly Valued by Company
Self-Restraint	_____	_____	_____
Working Memory	_____	_____	_____
Emotion Control	_____	_____	_____
Focus	_____	_____	_____
Task Initiation	_____	_____	_____
Planning/Prioritization	_____	_____	_____
Organization	_____	_____	_____
Time Management	_____	_____	_____
Defining/Achieving Goals	_____	_____	_____
Flexibility	_____	_____	_____
Observation	_____	_____	_____
Stress Tolerance	_____	_____	_____

INDEX